My
First Grade
Workbook

This book belongs to:

Riley

Way to Go!

After completing each activity, color a star to track how much you've done!

1 2 3 4

5 6 7 8 9 10

11 12 13 14 15 16

17 18 19 20 21 22

23 24 25 26 27 28

29	30	31	32	33	34
35	36	37	38	39	40
41	42	43	44	45	46
47	48	49	50	51	52
53	54	55	56	57	58
59	60	61	62	63	64
65	66	67	68	69	70

71 72 73 74 75 76

77 78 79 80 81 82

83 84 85 86 87 88

89 90 91 92 93 94

95 96 97 98 99 100

101

My
First Grade
Workbook

101
Games and Activities
to Support First Grade Skills

BRITTANY LYNCH

Illustrations by Robin Boyer

ROCKRIDGE
PRESS

Interior & Cover Designer: Liz Cosgrove
Art Producer: Sara Feinstein
Photo Art Director: Amy Burditt
Editor: Jeanine Le Ny
Production Editor: Andrew Yackira
Illustrations: © Robin Boyer, 2019.

ISBN: 978-1-64152-446-9

Contents

Note to Parents

Dear Parents,

First grade is a big year for kids. First graders are developing stronger social skills and becoming more independent and responsible, all while building upon the skills they learned in kindergarten. They are absorbing new academic skills in literacy, math, science, and social studies. By the end of first grade, they are stronger readers and blooming mathematicians.

My First Grade Workbook is designed to reinforce many of the skills your child is about to discover. Use it to give your child a boost before entering the classroom, to offer extra support at home while first grade is in session, or as a fun review over the summer so that newly learned skills stay fresh.

As a former elementary school teacher with a master's degree in early childhood education, I know what children need to be successful learners. Kids learn best when they are engaged in what they are doing. The 101 games and activities in this workbook were designed to keep kids entertained and motivated. Through coloring, mazes, search-and-find puzzles, and other fun games, children will practice essential first grade skills such as phonics, grammar, writing, numbers, math, science, and more—and they won't even realize they are learning!

The subjects are color-coded by section to make finding the material easy. Within each section, the activities start off simple and slowly increase in difficulty. Completing the easiest ones first will allow your child's confidence to build, and your child will quickly become curious and eager to see what comes next!

Children learn at different speeds, so it's okay if your child needs a little support when working through the book. Read the directions aloud and, if needed, help your child get started. If an activity seems to frustrate your child, skip that page, and try it again at another time. The goal of *My First Grade Workbook* is to support your child's first grade skills and to make learning fun.

So, let's go for it!

Brittany Lynch

1. Time for School

Help the fish get to school. Follow the path in alphabetical order from **a** to **z**.

a b c p h e
c m
i f o d e f a r
g
l h
w i j
b k d n x k
s l
s r q p o n m
t r
u v w x y z

2. Show What You Know: A, B, C

A a

Circle every **a** in the words.

apple   banana
candy   math
ask   awake

B b

Trace each word. Draw a line to the matching picture.

ball

bear

bug

C c

Color the pictures that begin with the letter **C**.

3. A Birthday Celebration

Put a ⬭ on 3 items that begin with **A**.

Put a ☐ on 3 items that begin with **B**.

Put a △ on 3 items that begin with **C**.

4. Show What You Know: D, E, F

Circle every D or d.

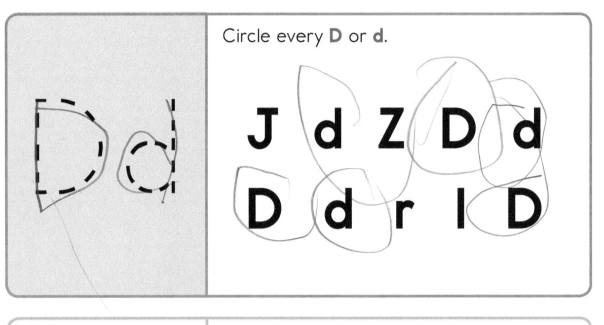

J d Z D d
D d r I D

Write the missing letter in each word.

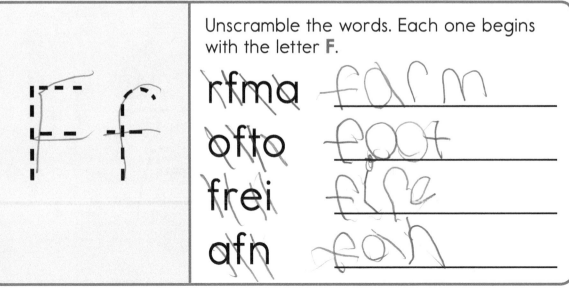

_envelope

_lephant

_gg

Unscramble the words. Each one begins with the letter F.

rfma — farm

ofto — foot

frei — fire

afn — fan

5. Be the Artist

Draw a picture on the easel that begins with the sound on the paint can.

6. Show What You Know: G, H, I

Circle every **g** in the words.

goat   game

leg   wiggle

gorilla   pig

G g

Trace each word. Draw a line to the matching picture.

hat

house

heart

H h

Color the pictures that begin with the letter **I**.

I i

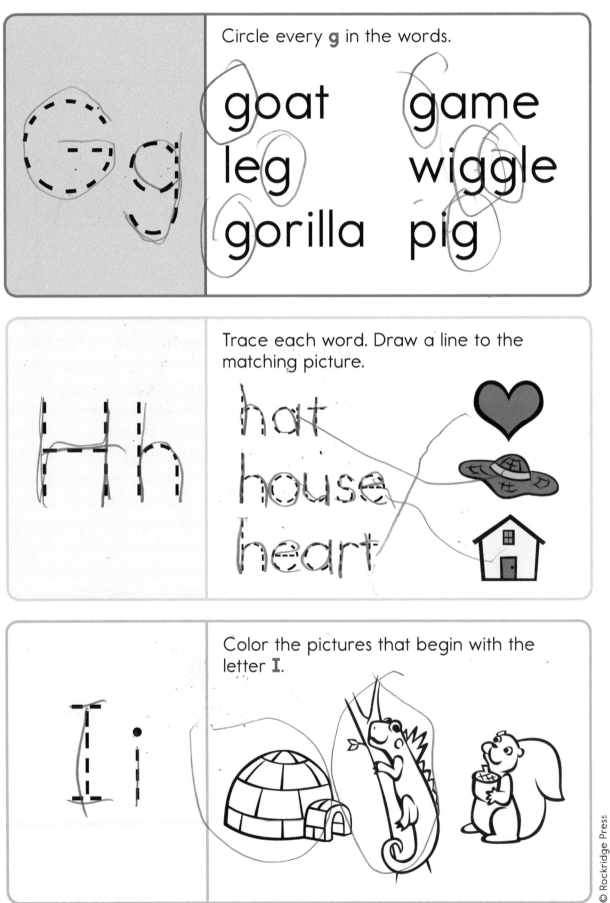

7. Let's Go Fishing!

Color the fish with uppercase letters **purple**. Color the fish with lowercase letters **yellow**.

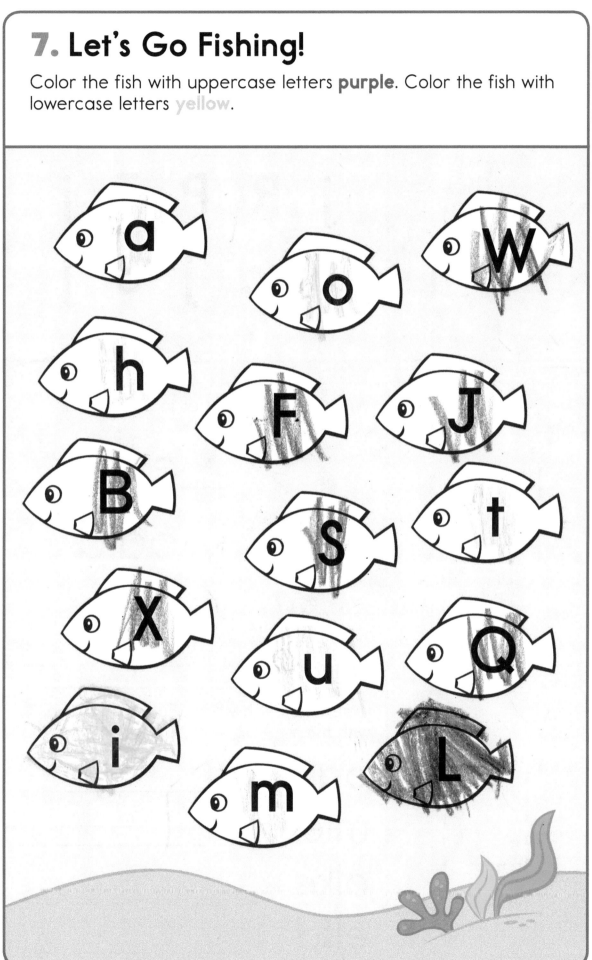

8. Show What You Know: J, K, L

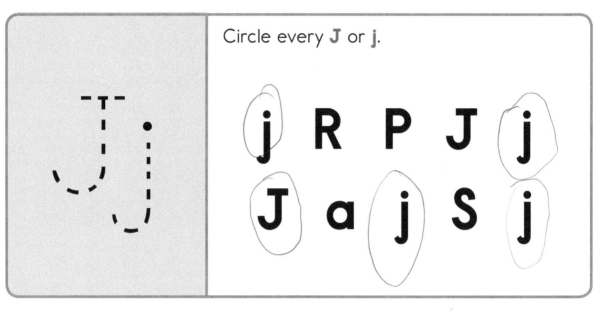

Circle every **J** or **j**.

j R P J j
J a j S j

Write the missing letter in each word.

_K_ey

_K_oala

_K_ing

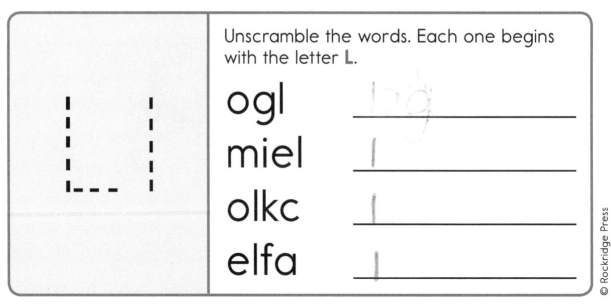

Unscramble the words. Each one begins with the letter **L**.

ogl _____

miel _____

olkc _____

elfa _____

My First Grade Workbook

9. Riddle Me This

Solve the riddles using the words from the word bank.

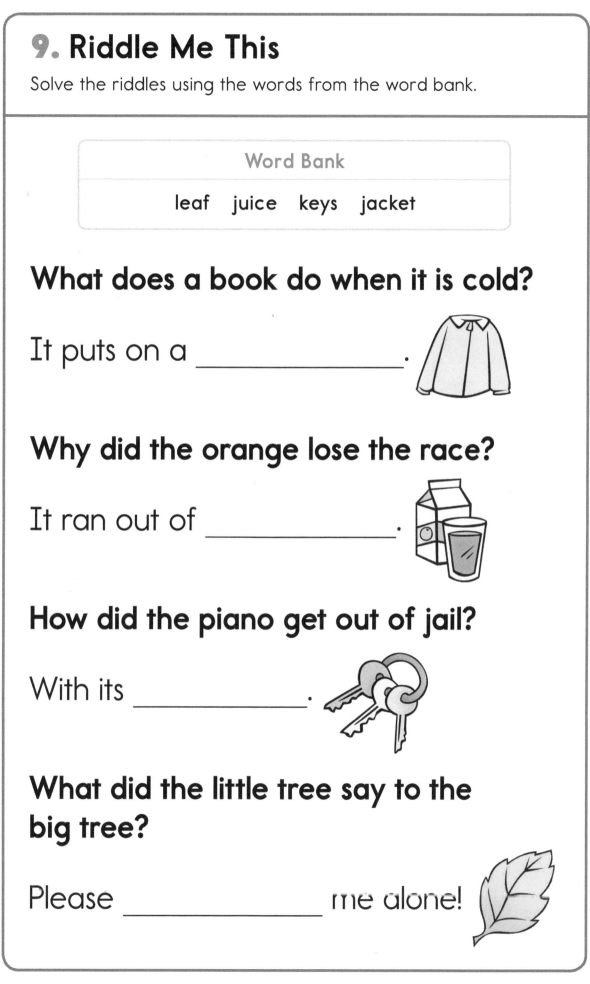

Word Bank
leaf   juice   keys   jacket

What does a book do when it is cold?

It puts on a _____.

Why did the orange lose the race?

It ran out of _____.

How did the piano get out of jail?

With its _____.

What did the little tree say to the big tree?

Please _____ me alone!

10. Show What You Know: M, N, O

Mm

Circle every **m** in the words.

ham   marker

lemon   monster

mom   camp

Nn

Trace each word. Draw a line to the matching picture.

nest

nail

nurse

Oo

Color the pictures that begin with the letter **O**.

11. Snack Time!

Help these hungry kids get their snacks. Complete each maze.

Follow the letters **M** and **m**.

Follow the letters **N** and **n**.

Follow the letters **O** and **o**.

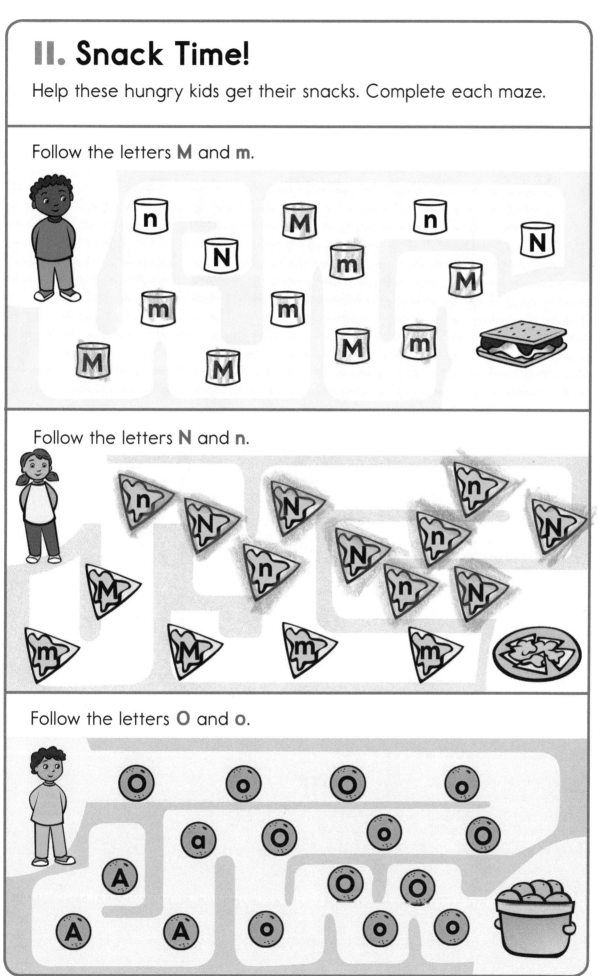

12. Show What You Know: P, Q, R

Pp

Circle every **P** and **p**.

P t p B p

P u p X P

Qq

Write the missing letter in each word.

__uarter

__uilt

__ueen

Rr

Unscramble the words. Each one begins with the letter **R**.

anir _____

igrn _____

atr _____

oers _____

13. A Healthy Treat

Use the color key to color the picture.

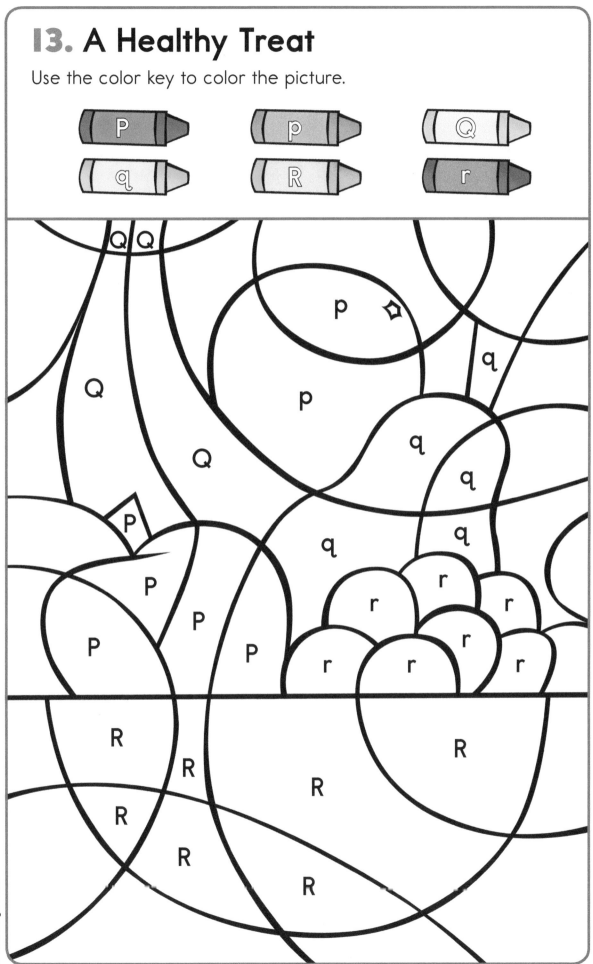

14. Show What You Know: S, T, U

Circle every **s** in the words.

sun   post

grass   fish

soup   shoes

Trace each word. Draw a line to the matching picture.

turtle

taco

tent

Color the pictures that begin with the letter **U**.

15. From Here to There

Find and circle the transportation words. Search across and down to solve the puzzle.

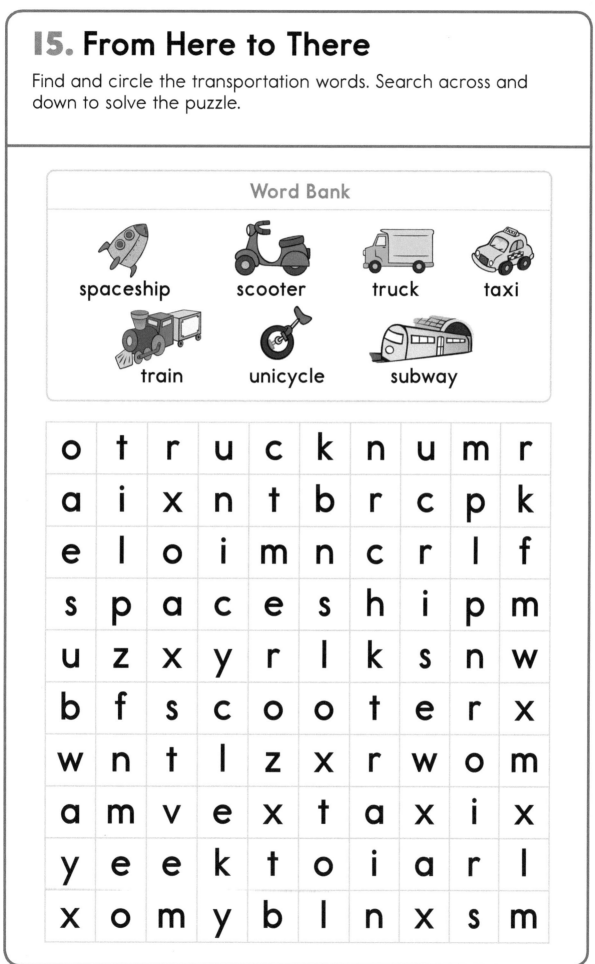

Word Bank

spaceship   scooter   truck   taxi

train   unicycle   subway

o	t	r	u	c	k	n	u	m	r
a	i	x	n	t	b	r	c	p	k
e	l	o	i	m	n	c	r	l	f
s	p	a	c	e	s	h	i	p	m
u	z	x	y	r	l	k	s	n	w
b	f	s	c	o	o	t	e	r	x
w	n	t	l	z	x	r	w	o	m
a	m	v	e	x	t	a	x	i	x
y	e	e	k	t	o	i	a	r	l
x	o	m	y	b	l	n	x	s	m

16. Show What You Know: V, W, X

Circle every **V** and **v**.

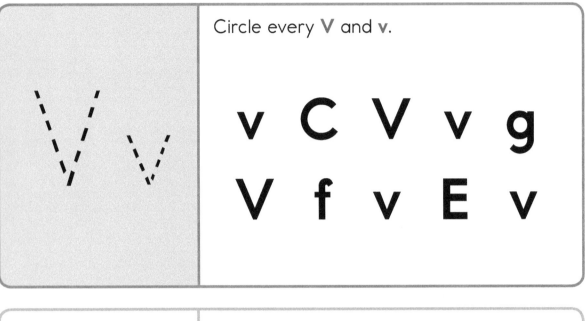

v C V v g
V f v E v

Write the missing letter in each word.

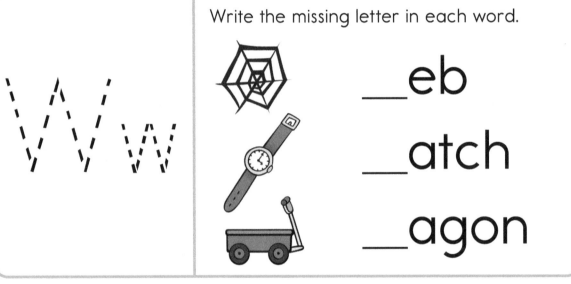

__eb

__atch

__agon

Unscramble the words. Each one ends with the letter **X**.

xwa _____

xsi _____

xo _____

imx _____

17. Cool Crossword

Use the picture clues and the word bank to complete the crossword puzzle.

Word Bank

van   vacuum   violin   window

waffle   wig   ax   mix   fox

18. Show What You Know: Y, Z

Y y

Circle every **y** in the words.

play   fly

yogurt   yes

yellow   yarn

yummy   hay

Z z

Trace each word. Draw a line to the matching picture.

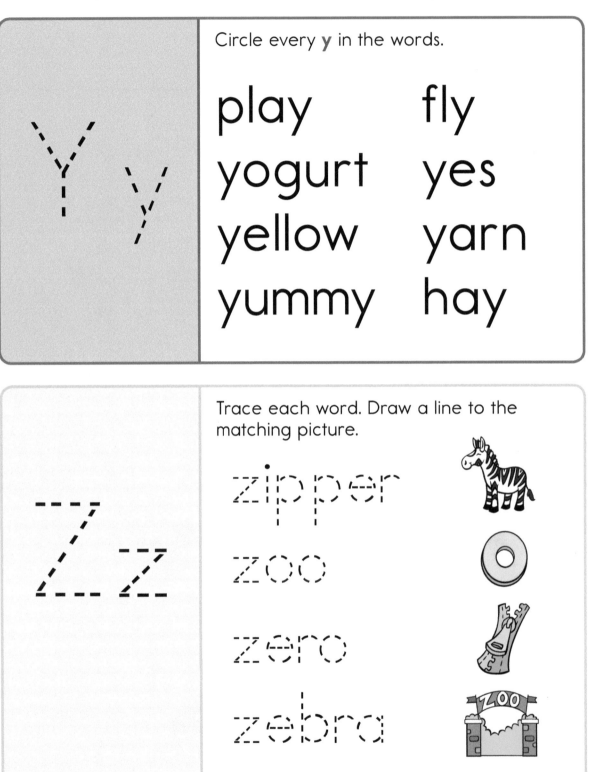

zipper

zoo

zero

zebra

19. High in the Sky

Start at the **red** star. Connect the dots with the letter **Y**.

Start at the **blue** star. Connect the dots with the letter **Z**.

20. Riddle at the Beach

Write the words in ABC order. Then unscramble the letters in the boxes to answer the riddle.

Word Bank

sand

umbrella

swimsuit

bucket

goggles

ocean

shell

towel

shovel

beach

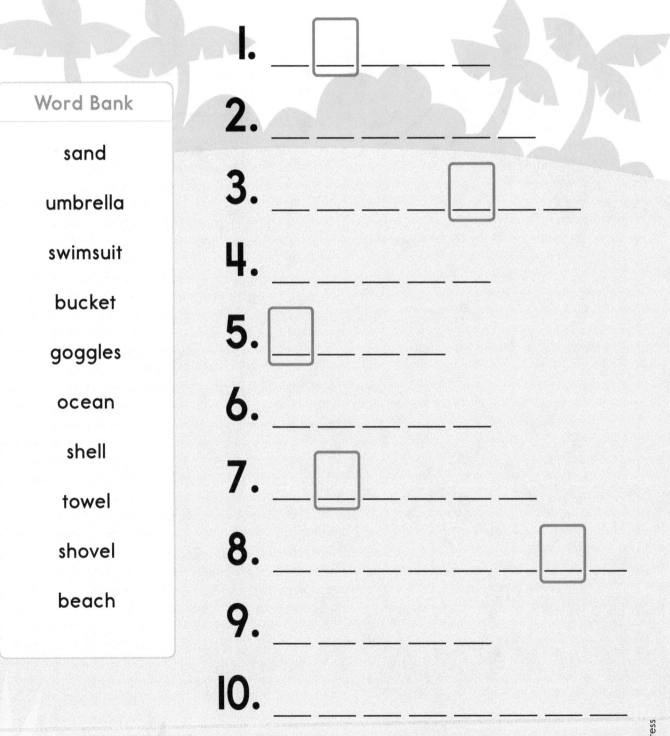

1. __ [ ] __ __ __

2. __ __ __ __ __ __ __ __

3. __ __ __ __ [ ] __ __

4. __ __ __ __ __ __

5. [ ] __ __ __ __

6. __ __ __ __ __ __ __

7. [ ] __ __ __ __ __

8. __ __ __ __ __ __ [ ] __

9. __ __ __ __ __

10. __ __ __ __ __ __ __ __

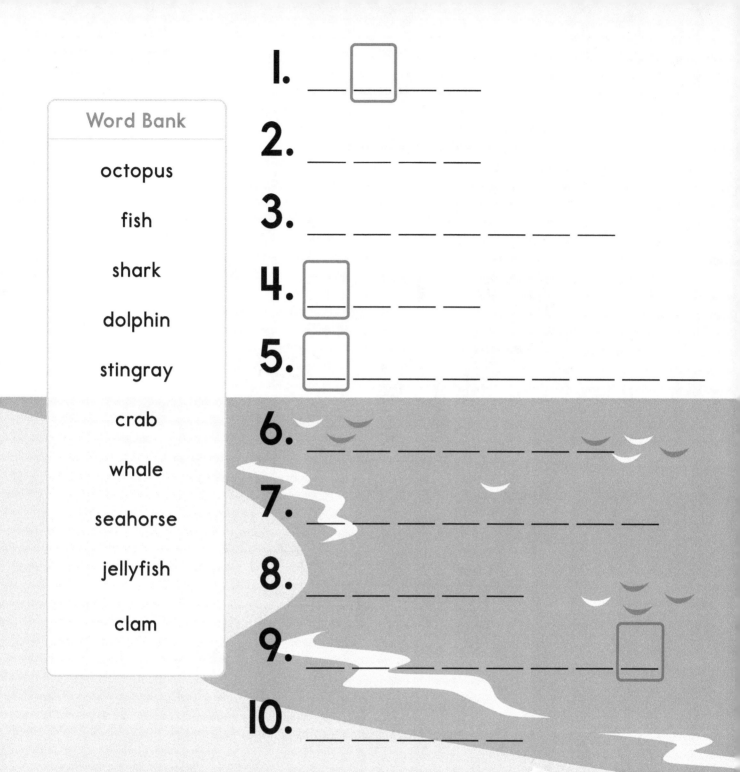

Word Bank

octopus

fish

shark

dolphin

stingray

crab

whale

seahorse

jellyfish

clam

1. ___ ☐ ___ ___

2. ___ ___ ___ ___

3. ___ ___ ___ ___ ___ ___ ___

4. ☐ ___ ___ ___ ___

5. ☐ ___ ___ ___ ___ ___ ___ ___

6. ___ ___ ___ ___ ___

7. ___ ___ ___ ___ ___

8. ___ ___ ___ ___ ___

9. ___ ___ ___ ___ ___ ___ ☐

10. ___ ___ ___ ___ ___

What fish tastes best with peanut butter?

___ ___ ___ ___ ___ ___ ___ ___ ___

21. Spring Syllables

How many syllables do you hear in each word? Cut and paste the correct number in each box.

3 4 1 2 3 2

22. Sailing Vowels

Use the color key to color the picture according to the short vowels in the words.

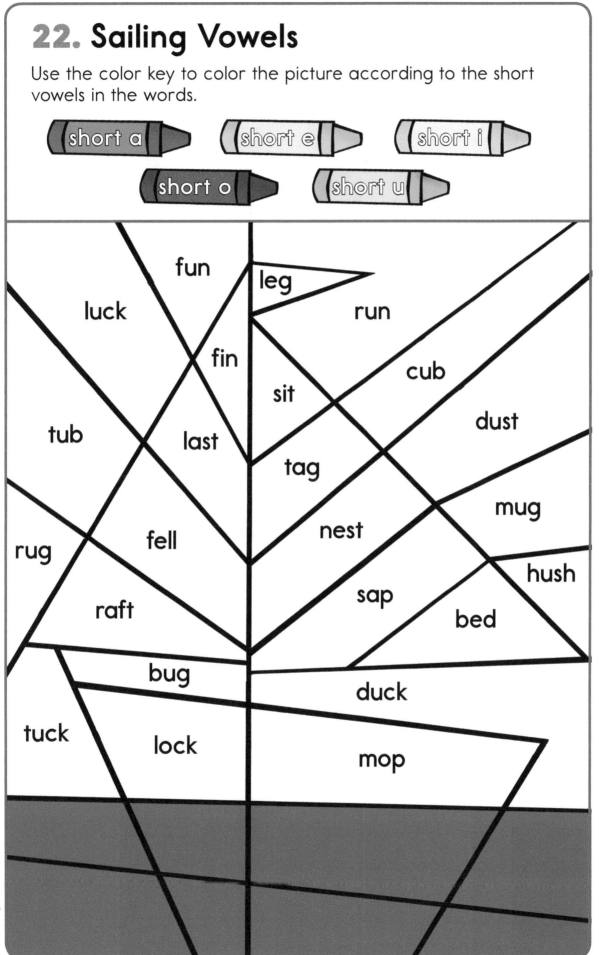

short a

short e

short i

short o

short u

fun

leg

luck

run

fin

cub

sit

tub

dust

last

tag

mug

fell

nest

hush

rug

sap

raft

bed

bug

duck

tuck

lock

mop

23. Simply Short Vowels

Write the word for each picture. Then use your answers to complete the crossword puzzle. Use the word bank to help.

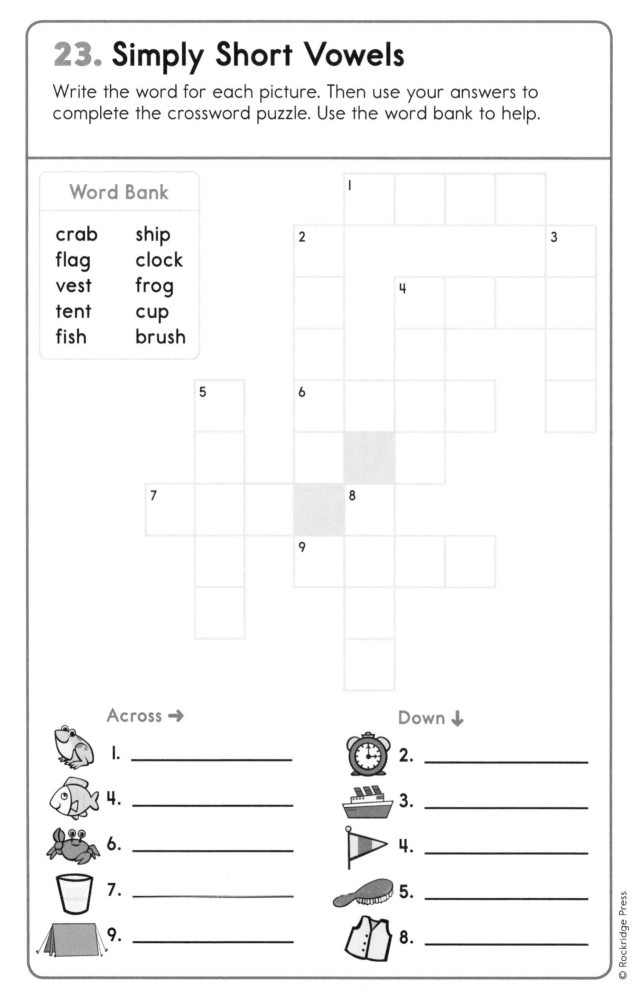

Word Bank

crab   ship
flag   clock
vest   frog
tent   cup
fish   brush

Across →

1. _____

4. _____

6. _____

7. _____

9. _____

Down ↓

2. _____

3. _____

4. _____

5. _____

8. _____

24. Leafy Long Vowels

Complete the maze. Color only the leaves that have **long vowel** words.

tube

cake

weed

line

name

cab

bat

step

ride

mend

tub

grab

bug

rock

mud

tie

mail

stop

bee

pay

math

cute

hike

crow

hope

road

seat

rate

note

© Rockridge Press

25. Blowing Bubbles

Color the consonants blue. Color the vowels pink.

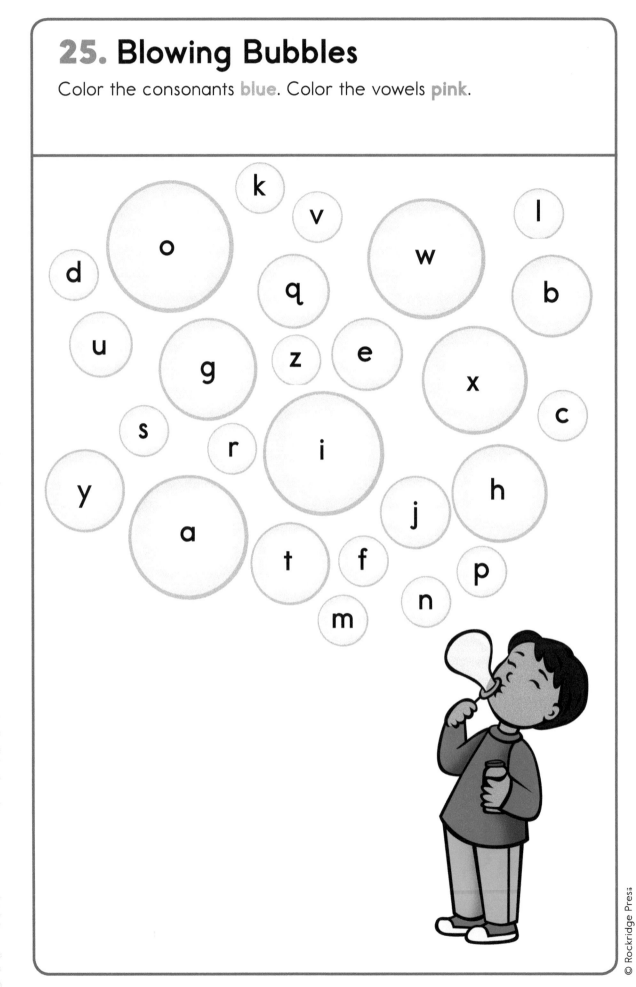

26. Crazy Coconuts!

Get through the maze safely. Follow the path that has only **consonants**.

27. What Doesn't Belong?

Say the digraph sound on the cookie jar. Say the name of the picture on each cookie. Put an ✗ on the one that does not belong.

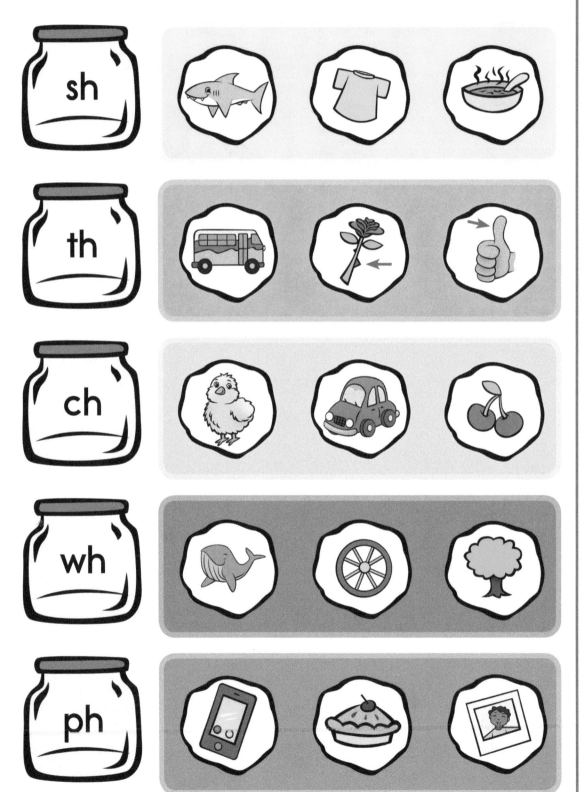

28. Match the Blends

Draw a line from each picture to its blend sound.

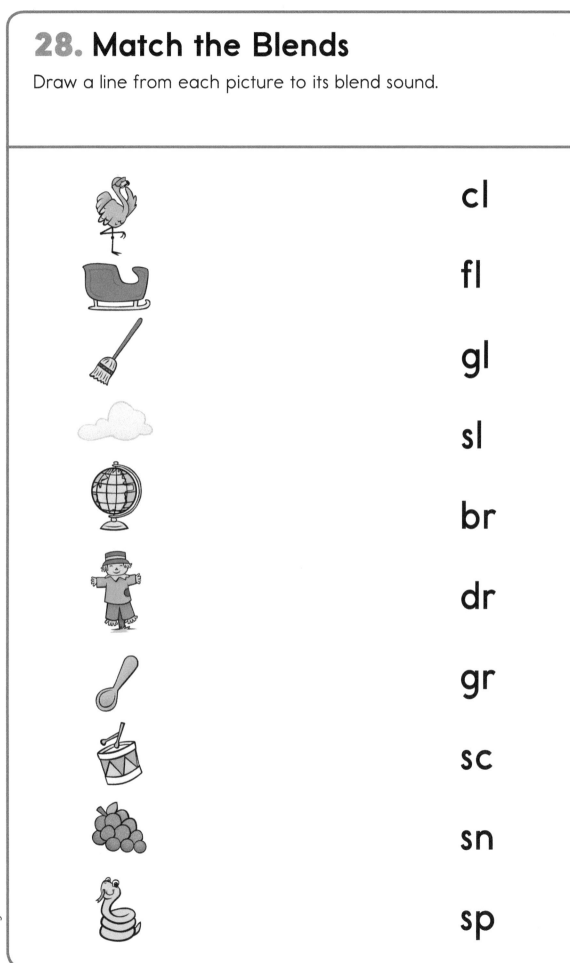

cl

fl

gl

sl

br

dr

gr

sc

sn

sp

29. Starry Nouns

Use the color key to color the stars.

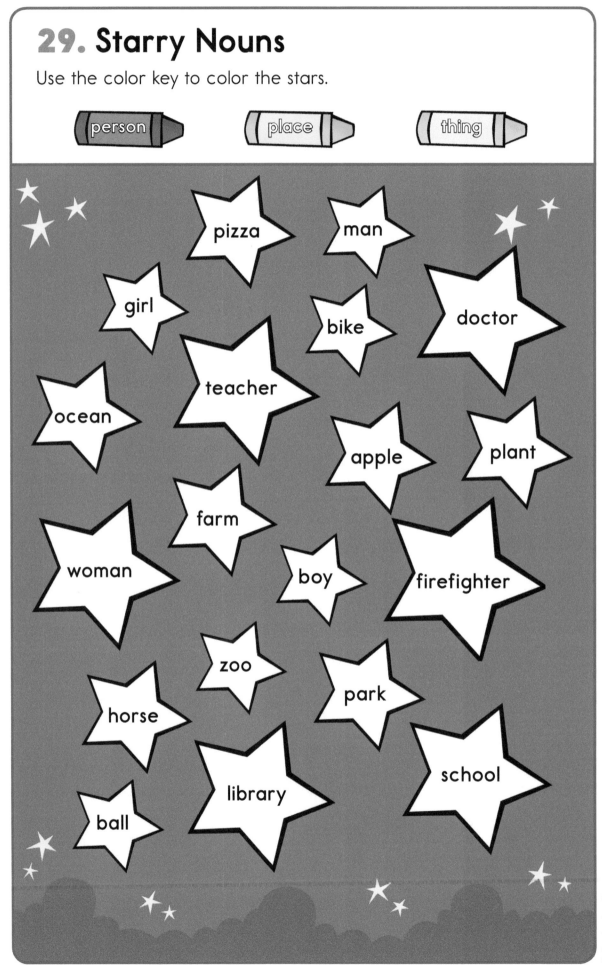

person

place

thing

pizza

man

girl

bike

doctor

teacher

ocean

apple

plant

farm

woman

boy

firefighter

zoo

park

horse

school

ball

library

30. Picking Tomatoes

Draw a line from each tomato to the correct basket.

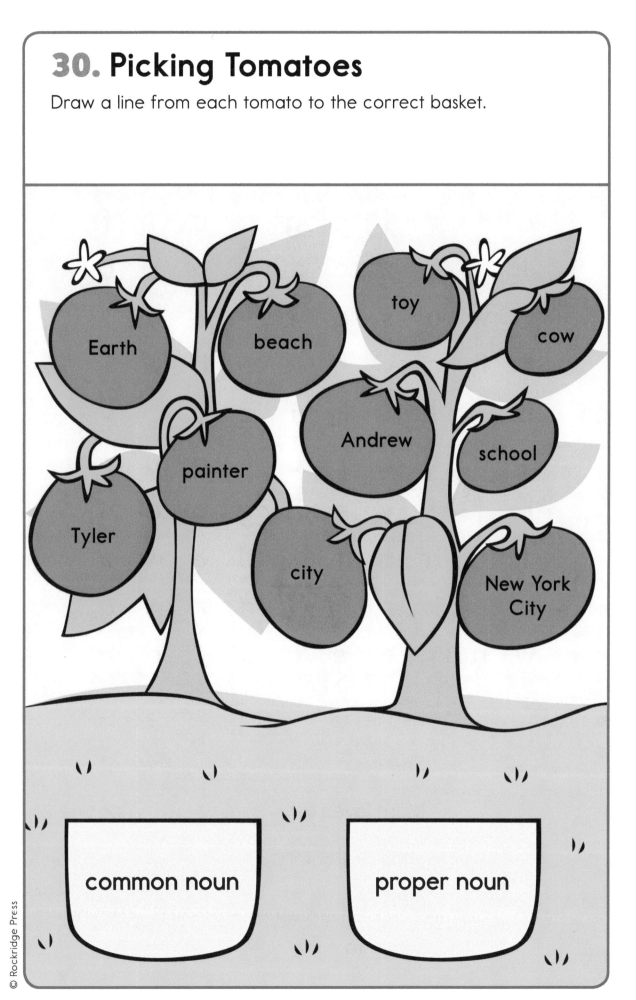

Earth   beach   toy   cow

painter   Andrew   school

Tyler   city   New York City

common noun   proper noun

31. Verb Action

Use the word bank to write the missing verb in each sentence. Then find and circle the words in the puzzle. Be sure to look across, down, and diagonally.

a	t	r	l	p	g	a	u	i	f
l	j	d	x	o	m	y	q	r	d
c	w	u	s	g	i	v	e	a	t
k	h	c	y	o	e	d	b	w	f
b	f	l	w	b	i	g	o	c	y
j	x	q	b	r	u	r	a	u	i
b	f	l	y	e	h	g	a	o	n
f	a	h	g	t	w	d	e	w	z
z	b	k	r	e	a	d	r	w	g
w	n	t	e	e	a	x	i	d	h

Word Bank

fly
eat
throw
read
ride
bake

He likes to _____ books.

She can _____ the ball.

Mom loves to _____ cookies.

Look at the bird _____.

Can you _____ a bike?

I love to _____ pizza!

32. Connect Four Verbs

Can you find **4** verbs in a row? Draw a line to connect them. Search across, down, and diagonally to solve the puzzle.

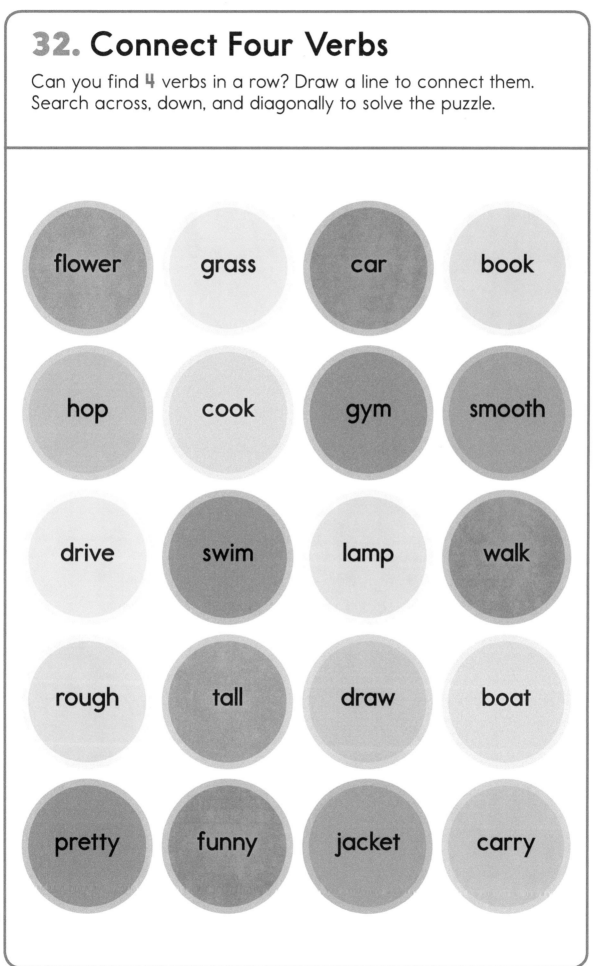

flower	grass	car	book
hop	cook	gym	smooth
drive	swim	lamp	walk
rough	tall	draw	boat
pretty	funny	jacket	carry

33. Amazing Adjectives

For each game below, draw a line through every adjective. Three in a row makes tic-tac-toe!

shoe	pencil	flower
build	carry	little
beautiful	silly	lazy

sad	milk	paint
dream	clean	brave
bird	dig	tiny

candy	school	cold
run	round	smart
itchy	listen	baby

home	snake	cut
soft	slimy	bumpy
dance	wash	messy

34. Acorn Adjectives

Find the acorns that have adjectives. Color them **brown**.

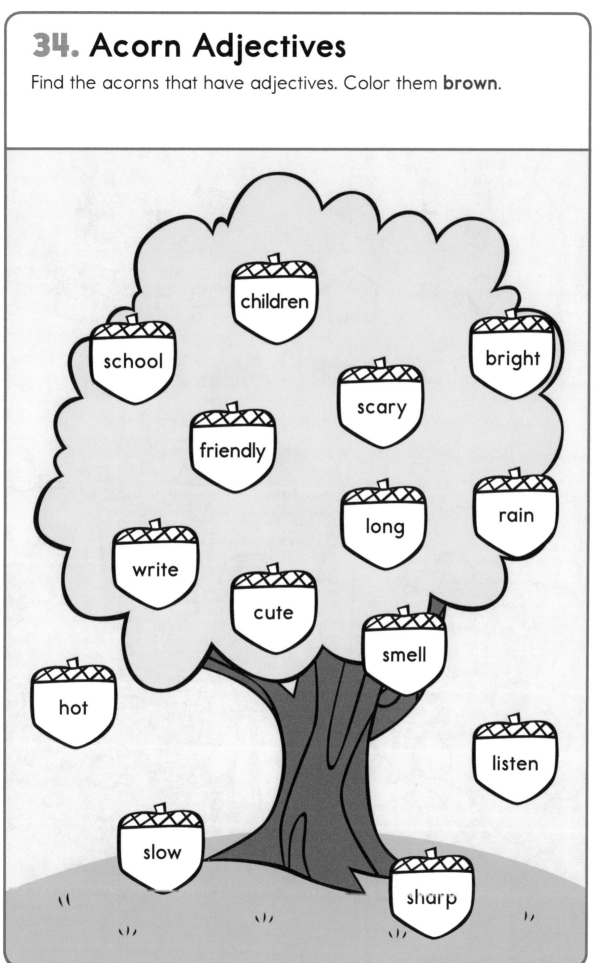

35. Compound Word Castle

Say the names of the pictures in each box. What compound words do they make? Find and circle the hidden pictures that match the compound words.

My First Grade Workbook

36. Building Compound Words

Draw a line to match each yellow sign with an orange sign that makes a compound word. Then find and circle the **5** compound words in the puzzle.

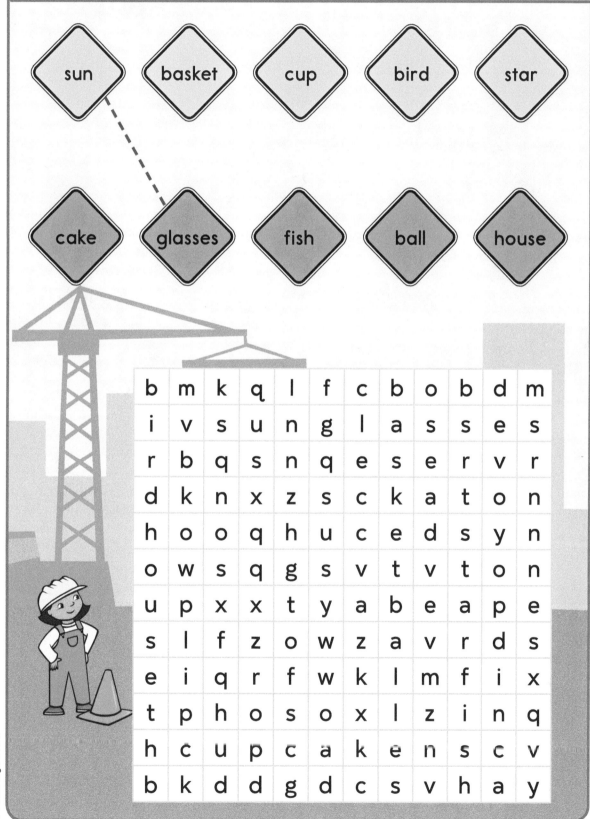

sun   basket   cup   bird   star

cake   glasses   fish   ball   house

b	m	k	q	l	f	c	b	o	b	d	m
i	v	s	u	n	g	l	a	s	s	e	s
r	b	q	s	n	q	e	s	e	r	v	r
d	k	n	x	z	s	c	k	a	t	o	n
h	o	o	q	h	u	c	e	d	s	y	n
o	w	s	q	g	s	v	t	v	t	o	n
u	p	x	x	t	y	a	b	e	a	p	e
s	l	f	z	o	w	z	a	v	r	d	s
e	i	q	r	f	w	k	l	m	f	i	x
t	p	h	o	s	o	x	l	z	i	n	q
h	c	u	p	c	a	k	e	n	s	c	v
b	k	d	d	g	d	c	s	v	h	a	y

37. Rhyming Rodeo

Solve the rhyming clues and complete the crossword puzzle. Use the word bank to help you.

Across →

1. Did you know the **king** could _____?

2. Was that **toy** for the _____?

3. Don't make a **peep**. Sam is trying to _____.

Down ↓

4. I can smell the **rose** with my _____.

5. Can you **hold** my _____?

6. The **goose** ran away from the _____.

(crossword grid)

2. b o y

Word Bank

moose sing boy nose sleep gold

38. Rhyme in a Row

For each game, draw a line through the pictures or words that rhyme. Three in a row makes tic-tac-toe!

pine	fine	line
dine	ball	rake
vest	pin	tire

leg	cash	hen
den	men	dice
pen	goat	pole

39. Penguin in Pajamas

Write in the missing words to complete the story.

Peggy the Penguin goes to bed at

_____. It's time to put on her
   [time]

_____ pajamas. They are her
   [color]

favorite. They feel _____.
                         [adjective]

She will _____ her teeth,
              [verb]

read a _____, and then go
              [noun]

to sleep.

My First Grade Workbook

40. Blake Bakes

Write in the missing words to complete the story.

First, Blake adds the brownie mix

and _____ to a bowl. Then he
[noun]

adds _____, and _____
[noun]   [verb]

it all together with a spoon. He pours

the batter into a _____ and puts
[noun]

it into the oven for _____ minutes.
[number]

When he opens the oven, he doesn't

see brownies, he finds _____
[adjective]

_____ instead!
[noun]

41. Funny Friday

Read the story. Then circle the answer to each question.

On Friday my teacher forgot to wear her glasses. She came to school with two different shoes on and her shirt on backward. Then she tried to write on the board with a glue stick! Next she picked up a lunch box and tried to read it to us. Thankfully, her sister brought her glasses at lunchtime. It sure was a funny Friday!

1. **What did the teacher try to read?**

   a) book   b) lunch box   c) newspaper

2. **Who brought the teacher her glasses?**

   a) dad   b) sister   c) mom

3. **What did the teacher try to do with the glue stick?**

   a) cut   b) write   c) glue

4. **What did the teacher wear backward?**

   a) shirt   b) shoes   c) pants

42. Disappearing Dinosaur

Read the story. Then write the answer to each question.

This morning I looked out my window. Can you guess what I saw? A dinosaur! It had on my favorite blue shorts. The dinosaur had my scooter. He did cool tricks. He could jump, spin, and ride backward! I ran to get my mom. When we came back, the dinosaur was gone.

1. What was the dinosaur wearing?

   _____

2. What did the dinosaur do tricks on?

   _____

3. What tricks could the dinosaur do?

   _____

4. Who did the boy try to show the dinosaur to?

   _____

43. Snow Fun

Read the story. Answer the questions.

It's snowing! Katie and Will can't wait to go outside to play. They put on their warm winter coats. Next Katie grabs a scarf, hat, buttons, and a carrot. Will finds two stones and two sticks. They start packing the snow. They make a small, medium, and large snowball.

What do you think will happen next?

_____

_____

Draw your prediction.

Why do you think so?

_____

_____

_____

44. You're the Author!

Write a story about the picture. Make sure your story has a beginning, middle, and end.

45. Counting Candy

Help Carter collect candy. Write in the missing numbers.

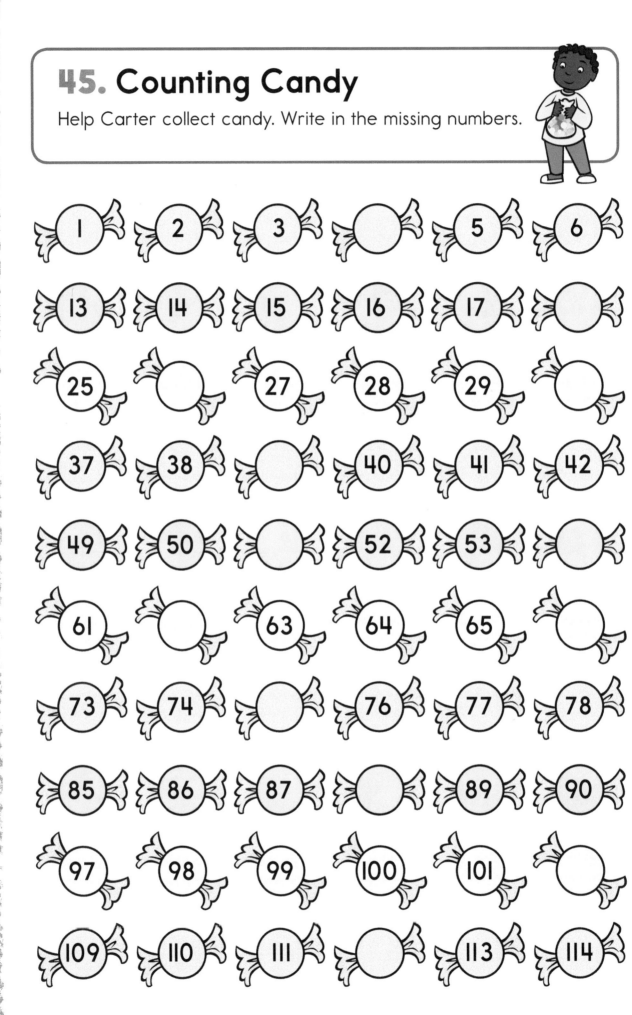

1 2 3 ☐ 5 6

13 14 15 16 17 ☐

25 ☐ 27 28 29 ☐

37 38 ☐ 40 41 42

49 50 ☐ 52 53 ☐

61 ☐ 63 64 65 ☐

73 74 ☐ 76 77 78

85 86 87 ☐ 89 90

97 98 99 100 101 ☐

109 110 111 ☐ 113 114

My First Grade Workbook

© Rockridge Press

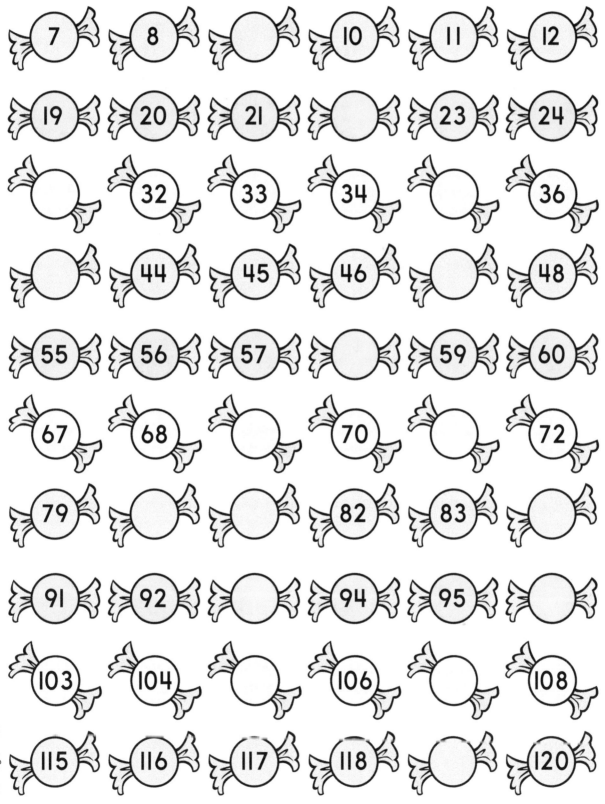

7	8		10	11	12
19	20	21		23	24
	32	33	34		36
	44	45	46		48
55	56	57		59	60
67	68		70		72
79			82	83	
91	92		94	95	
103	104		106		108
115	116	117	118		120

46. At the Zoo

How many of each animal do you see? Write the numbers in the boxes below.

My First Grade Workbook

47. Counting Shapes

Count the number of shapes in each box. Color the circle that has that number.

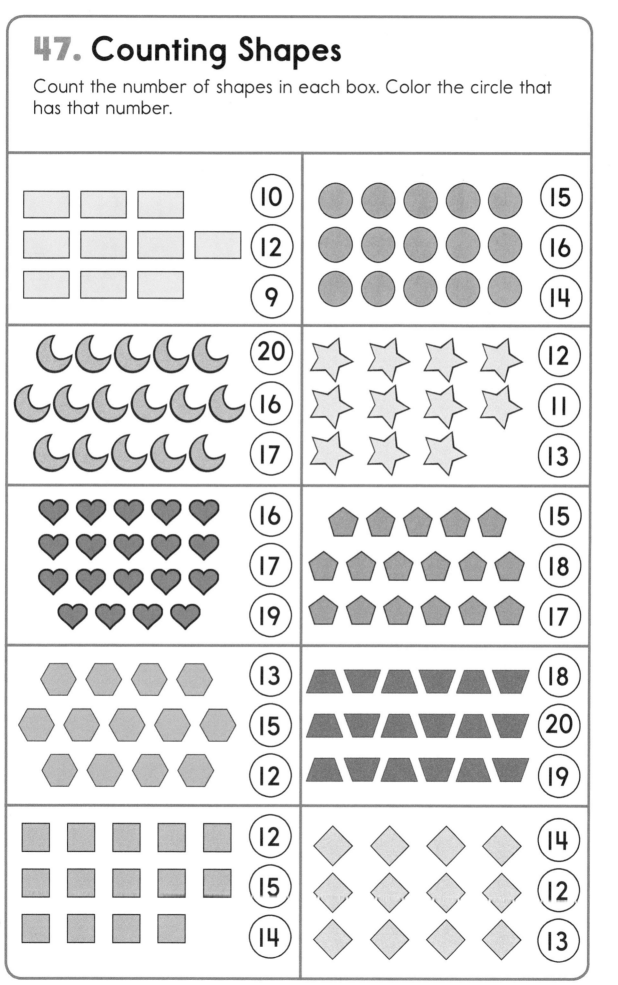

© Rockridge Press

48. Odd Numbers for Todd

Follow the path of only **odd** numbers to help Farmer Todd reach his tractor.

1	4	7	8	1	4	3	9
7	0	2	8	5	0	7	0
5	9	3	1	6	3	8	6
2	8	6	7	4	7	1	5
6	4	0	5	2	9	2	4
5	3	8	1	3	6	0	3
2	7	8	2	9	5	5	2
1	0	9	6	4	8	3	7

49. Hidden Numbers

Can you find **5** even numbers, between **1** and **20**, hidden in Emily's room?

I found these even numbers: ☐ ☐ ☐ ☐ ☐

50. Skip Through the Mazes

Skip count as fast as you can to complete the mazes.

Skip count by **2**s.

2   12   13   15
4   14
10   16
9   5
6   18   20
7   8

Skip count by **5**s.

25   60 65   81   79
                         78
20 30 55 70 75   76   77
5   10
15 35 50 71 80 95
18 17 16 40 45 72 85 90 100

Skip count by **10**s.

31   32   33   34
                      35
39   38   37   36
10 30 50 60 70
51   80
20 40 52 90   100

51. Skip Count and Color

Skip count by **5**s up to **100**. Find and color those numbers **yellow** as you count.

52. Sandy Surprise

What did the kids build at the beach? To find out, count to 100 by connecting each dot with a number that is **greater than** the one before.

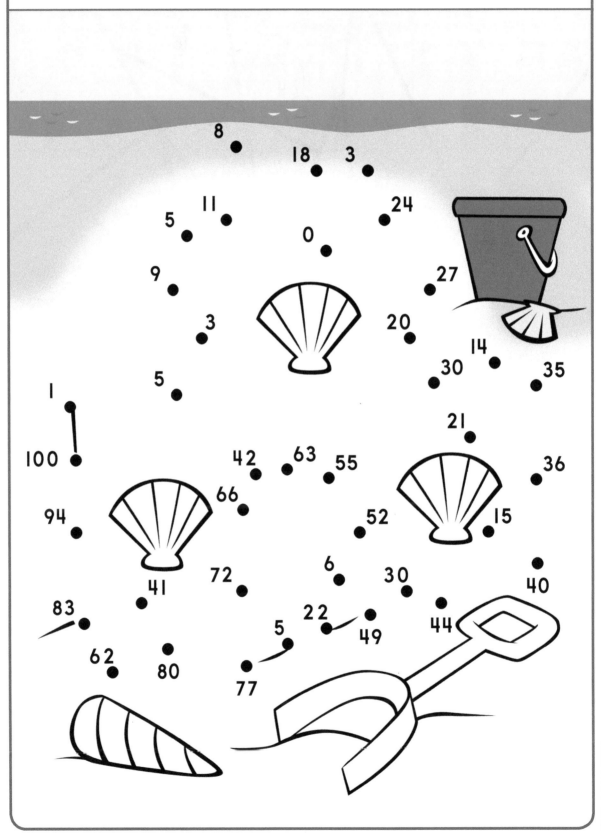

53. Lunch Vote!

The class voted on their favorite lunch. Use the bar graph to answer the questions below.

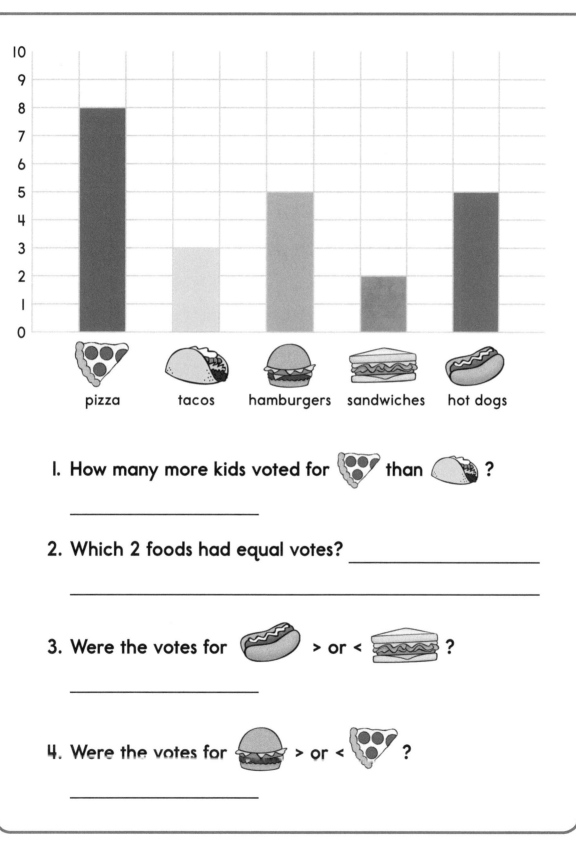

1. How many more kids voted for 🍕 than 🌮 ?

   _____

2. Which 2 foods had equal votes? _____

   _____

3. Were the votes for 🌭 > or < 🥪 ?

   _____

4. Were the votes for 🍔 > or < 🍕 ?

   _____

54. Comparing Capacity

Circle the object in each box that holds **more**. Then hunt for your answers in the word search. Be sure to look across, up, down, and diagonally.

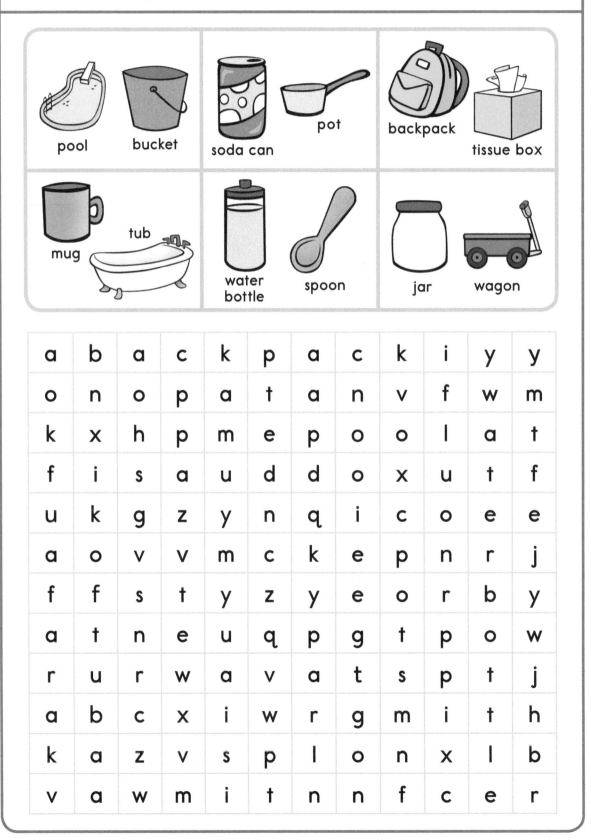

pool   bucket   soda can   pot   backpack   tissue box

mug   tub   water bottle   spoon   jar   wagon

a	b	a	c	k	p	a	c	k	i	y	y
o	n	o	p	a	t	a	n	v	f	w	m
k	x	h	p	m	e	p	o	o	l	a	t
f	i	s	a	u	d	d	o	x	u	t	f
u	k	g	z	y	n	q	i	c	o	e	e
a	o	v	v	m	c	k	e	p	n	r	j
f	f	s	t	y	z	y	e	o	r	b	y
a	t	n	e	u	q	p	g	t	p	o	w
r	u	r	w	a	v	a	t	s	p	t	j
a	b	c	x	i	w	r	g	m	i	t	h
k	a	z	v	s	p	l	o	n	x	l	b
v	a	w	m	i	t	n	n	f	c	e	r

55. Measuring School Supplies

How long is each item? Write your answers on the lines.

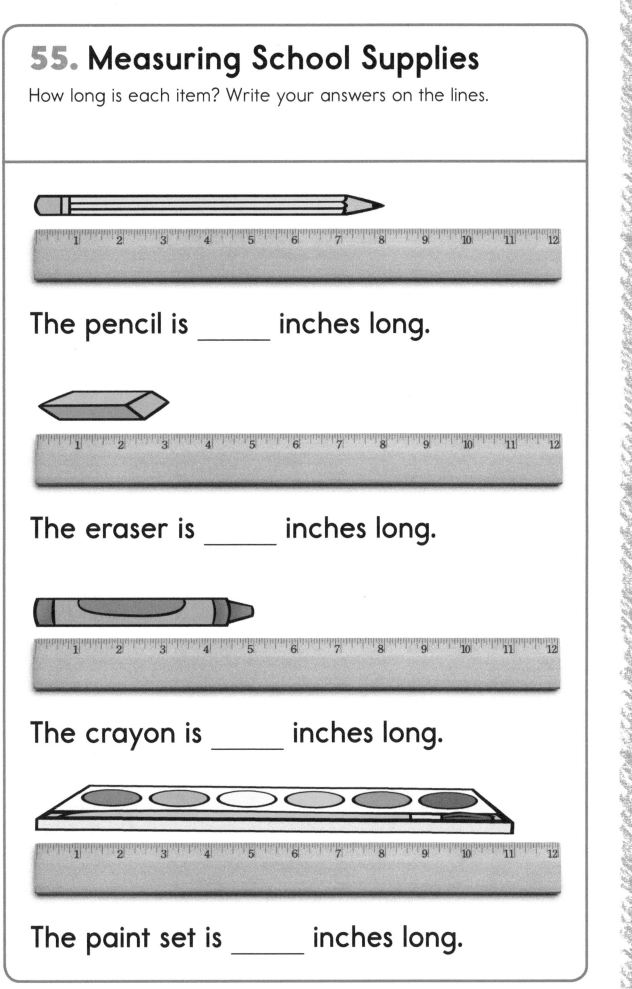

The pencil is _____ inches long.

The eraser is _____ inches long.

The crayon is _____ inches long.

The paint set is _____ inches long.

56. What's for Breakfast?

Use the color key to color the picture according to the place value of each number.

3 ones **2 tens**

9 ones **5 tens**

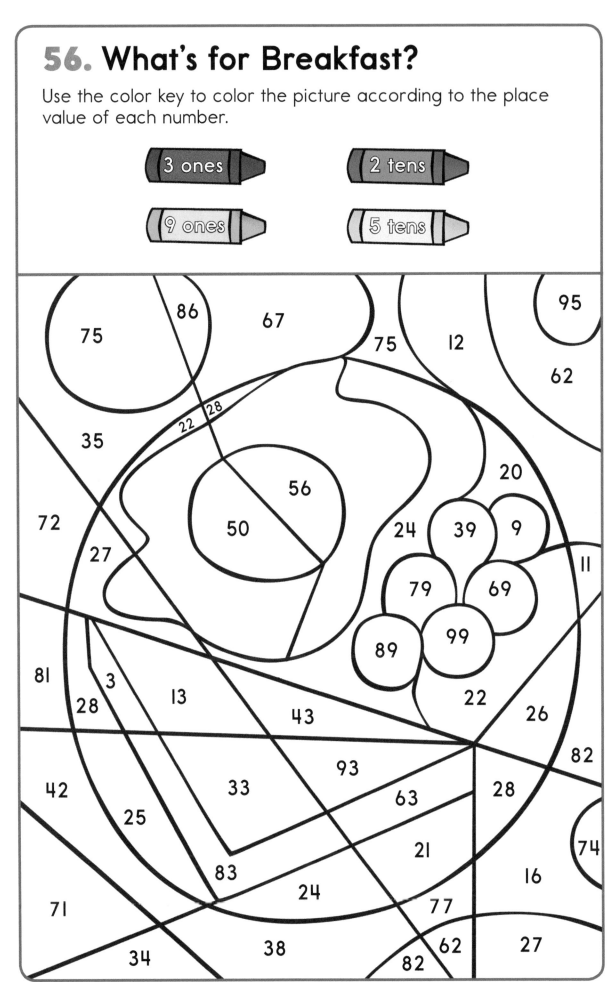

57. Pirate Place Value

Help the pirate find his treasure. Write in how many **tens** and **ones** are in each number.

58. Making Pizza

Look at the fraction. Draw toppings **only** on that part of the pizza.

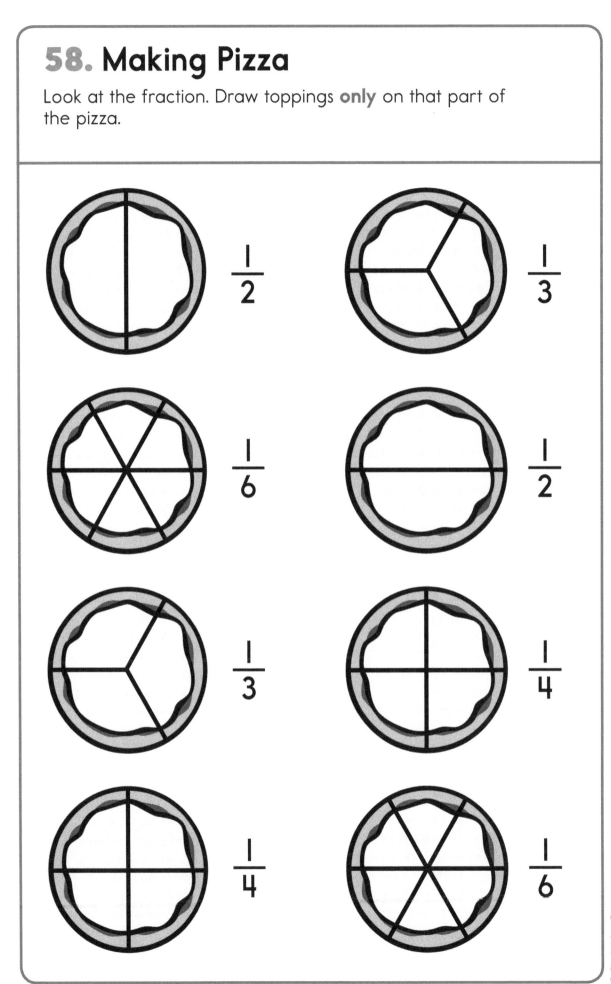

My First Grade Workbook

59. Fun with Fractions

Cut and paste the fractions in the correct boxes.

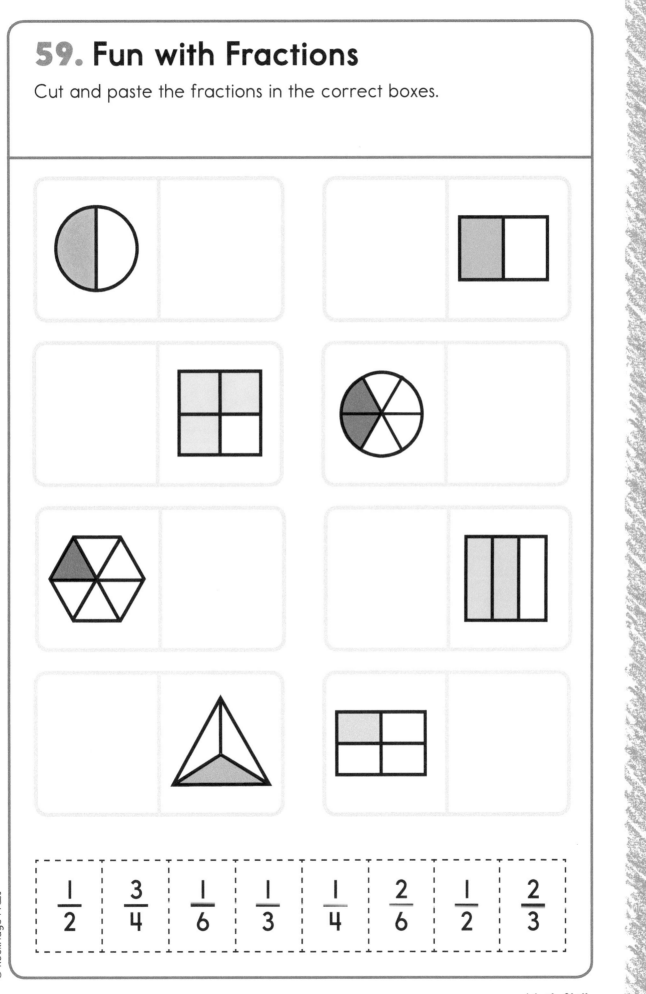

60. Who Stole the Cheese?

Solve each addition fact. Then connect the dots from **1** to **10** to see the sneaky thief.

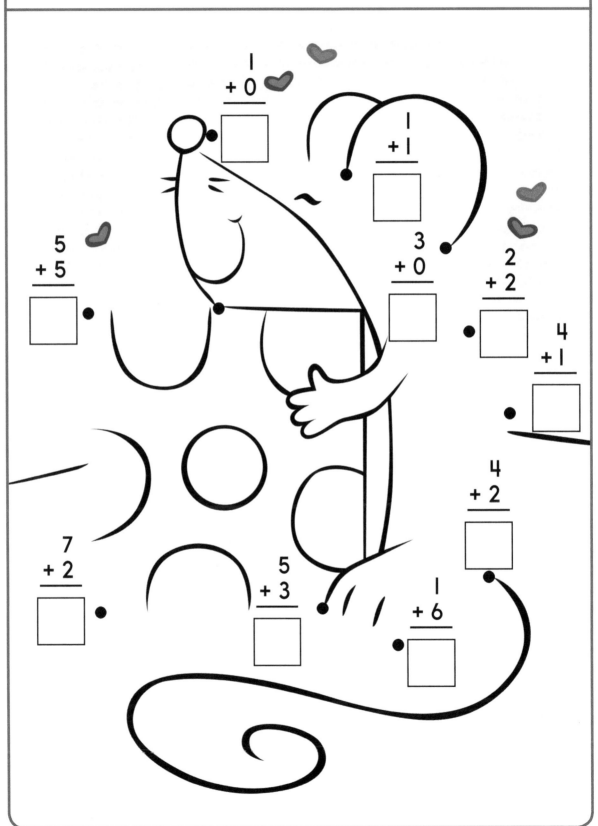

My First Grade Workbook

61. Colorful Addition

Solve the math facts. Use the color key to color the picture.

11 13 15
12 14 16

$$\begin{array}{r} 4 \\ +8 \\ \hline \end{array}$$

$$\begin{array}{r} 9 \\ +3 \\ \hline \end{array}$$

$$\begin{array}{r} 6 \\ +6 \\ \hline \end{array}$$

$$\begin{array}{r} 6 \\ +7 \\ \hline \end{array}$$

$$\begin{array}{r} 5 \\ +7 \\ \hline \end{array}$$

$$\begin{array}{r} 8 \\ +8 \\ \hline \end{array}$$

$$\begin{array}{r} 7 \\ +7 \\ \hline \end{array}$$

$$\begin{array}{r} 6 \\ +9 \\ \hline \end{array}$$

$$\begin{array}{r} 3 \\ +9 \\ \hline \end{array}$$

$$\begin{array}{r} 7 \\ +9 \\ \hline \end{array}$$

$$\begin{array}{r} 5 \\ +8 \\ \hline \end{array}$$

$$\begin{array}{r} 7 \\ +8 \\ \hline \end{array}$$

$$\begin{array}{r} 9 \\ +5 \\ \hline \end{array}$$

$$\begin{array}{r} 8 \\ +7 \\ \hline \end{array}$$

$$\begin{array}{r} 7 \\ +5 \\ \hline \end{array}$$

$$\begin{array}{r} 5 \\ +6 \\ \hline \end{array}$$

62. A Sea of Sums

Solve the math problems. Then find and circle the sums hidden in the ocean.

1 4 +0	8 2 +4	5 3 +2	9 1 +3	2 8 +6	7 3 +5	0 5 +1	8 6 +3

63. Submarine Math

Solve the math facts. Use the color key to circle the sums.

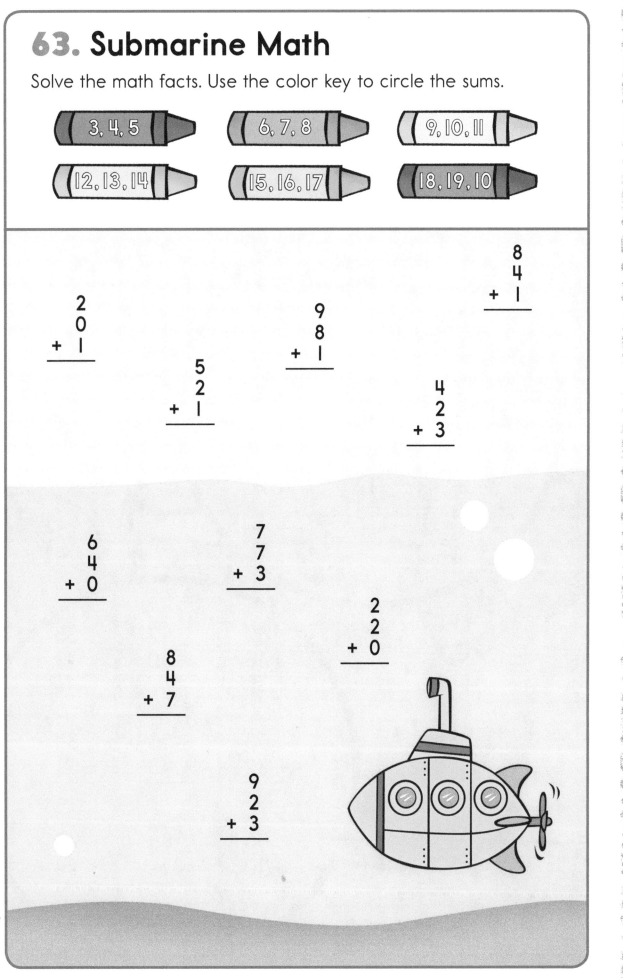

crayon	crayon	crayon
3, 4, 5	6, 7, 8	9, 10, 11
12, 13, 14	15, 16, 17	18, 19, 10

$$\begin{array}{r} 8 \\ 4 \\ +\ 1 \\ \hline \end{array}$$

$$\begin{array}{r} 2 \\ 0 \\ +\ 1 \\ \hline \end{array}$$

$$\begin{array}{r} 9 \\ 8 \\ +\ 1 \\ \hline \end{array}$$

$$\begin{array}{r} 5 \\ 2 \\ +\ 1 \\ \hline \end{array}$$

$$\begin{array}{r} 4 \\ 2 \\ +\ 3 \\ \hline \end{array}$$

$$\begin{array}{r} 6 \\ 4 \\ +\ 0 \\ \hline \end{array}$$

$$\begin{array}{r} 7 \\ 7 \\ +\ 3 \\ \hline \end{array}$$

$$\begin{array}{r} 2 \\ 2 \\ +\ 0 \\ \hline \end{array}$$

$$\begin{array}{r} 8 \\ 4 \\ +\ 7 \\ \hline \end{array}$$

$$\begin{array}{r} 9 \\ 2 \\ +\ 3 \\ \hline \end{array}$$

64. Turtle Tic-Tac-Toe

Solve the math problems. Draw a line through the matching sums. Three in a row makes tic-tac-toe!

63 + 14	30 + 33	29 + 10
12 + 55	78 + 11	25 + 21
35 + 23	12 + 46	37 + 21

62 + 16	42 + 30	35 + 31
53 + 32	23 + 43	34 + 21
56 + 10	86 + 11	45 + 24

65. Connect 4 Calculations

Can you find **4** matching sums in a row? Draw a line to connect them. Search across, down, and diagonally to solve the puzzle.

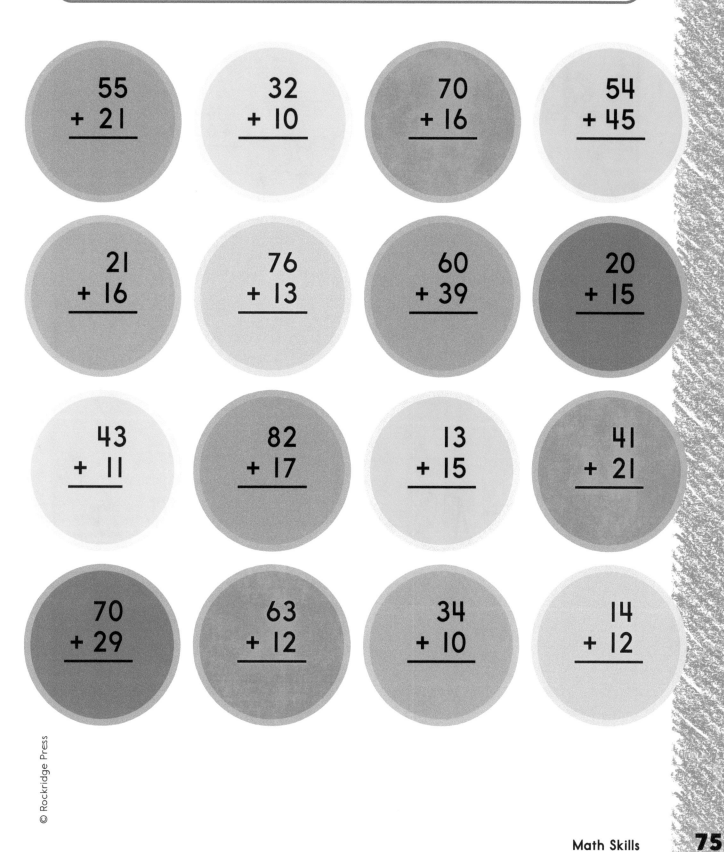

55
+ 21

32
+ 10

70
+ 16

54
+ 45

21
+ 16

76
+ 13

60
+ 39

20
+ 15

43
+ 11

82
+ 17

13
+ 15

41
+ 21

70
+ 29

63
+ 12

34
+ 10

14
+ 12

66. Addition Avenue

Follow the correct path to get the kids to school. Solve the math facts as you go.

$$\begin{array}{r} 0 \\ + 3 \\ \hline \end{array}$$

$$\begin{array}{r} 1 \\ + 1 \\ \hline \end{array}$$

$$\begin{array}{r} 16 \\ + 0 \\ \hline \end{array}$$

$$\begin{array}{r} 7 \\ + 1 \\ \hline \end{array}$$

$$\begin{array}{r} 21 \\ + 2 \\ \hline \end{array}$$

$$\begin{array}{r} 4 \\ + 1 \\ \hline \end{array}$$

$$\begin{array}{r} 13 \\ + 8 \\ \hline \end{array}$$

$$\begin{array}{r} 23 \\ + 1 \\ \hline \end{array}$$

$$\begin{array}{r} 8 \\ + 3 \\ \hline \end{array}$$

$$\begin{array}{r} 6 \\ + 7 \\ \hline \end{array}$$

$$\begin{array}{r} 10 \\ + 5 \\ \hline \end{array}$$

$$\begin{array}{r} 14 \\ + 3 \\ \hline \end{array}$$

$$\begin{array}{r} 9 \\ + 12 \\ \hline \end{array}$$

$$\begin{array}{r} 16 \\ + 0 \\ \hline \end{array}$$

$$\begin{array}{r} 29 \\ + 1 \\ \hline \end{array}$$

$$\begin{array}{r} 26 \\ + 3 \\ \hline \end{array}$$

$$\begin{array}{r} 15 \\ + 4 \\ \hline \end{array}$$

$$\begin{array}{r} 11 \\ + 7 \\ \hline \end{array}$$

$$\begin{array}{r} 10 \\ + 10 \\ \hline \end{array}$$

67. Sum Riddle

Solve the sums. Then use the code to answer the riddle.

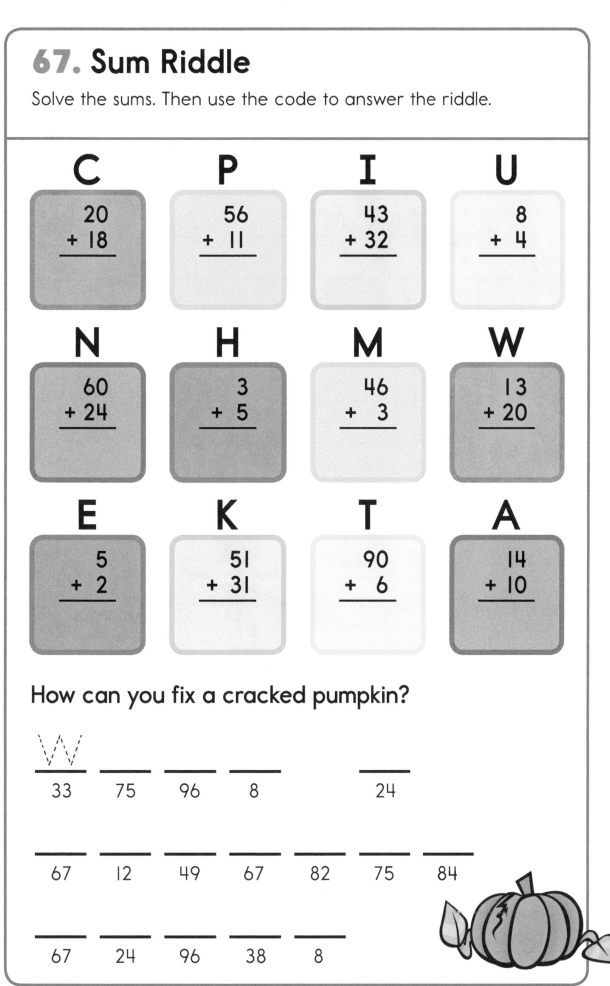

C
20
+ 18
___

P
56
+ 11
___

I
43
+ 32
___

U
8
+ 4
___

N
60
+ 24
___

H
3
+ 5
___

M
46
+ 3
___

W
13
+ 20
___

E
5
+ 2
___

K
51
+ 31
___

T
90
+ 6
___

A
14
+ 10
___

How can you fix a cracked pumpkin?

W̲ ___ ___ ___   ___
33   75   96   8   24

___ ___ ___ ___ ___ ___ ___
67   12   49   67   82   75   84

___ ___ ___ ___ ___
67   24   96   38   8

68. School Supply Subtraction

Solve the math facts. Then use the color key to color the picture.

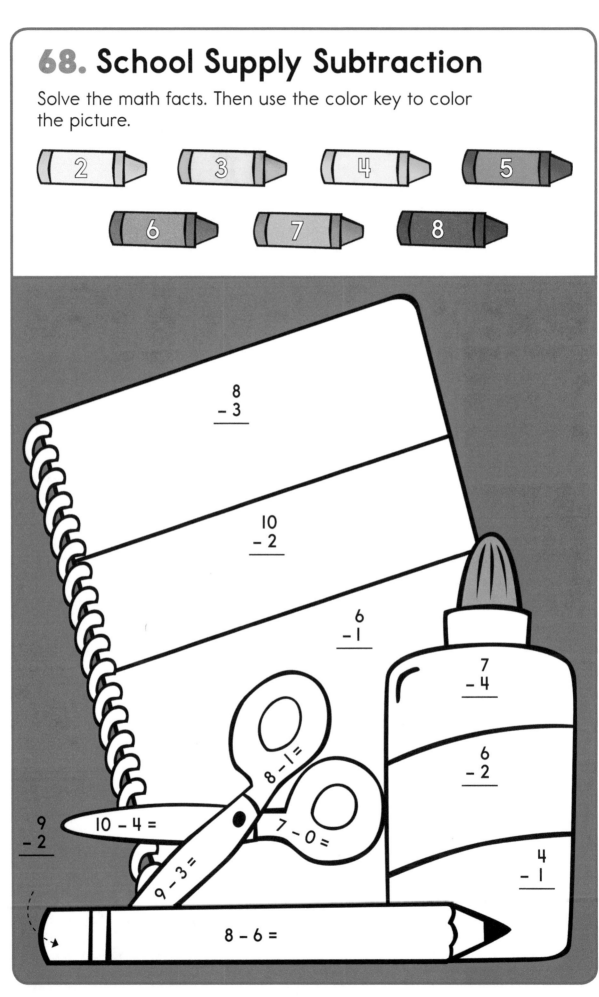

2 3 4 5

6 7 8

8
− 3

10
− 2

6
− 1

7
− 4

6
− 2

9
− 2

8 − 1 =

10 − 4 =

7 − 0 =

9 − 3 =

− 4
− 1

8 − 6 =

69. Superhero Tic-Tac-Toe

Circle the math problems that have the correct answer. Put an X on the ones that have the wrong answer. Three in a row makes tic-tac-toe!

$\begin{array}{r} 9 \\ -4 \\ \hline 5 \end{array}$	$\begin{array}{r} 4 \\ -0 \\ \hline 3 \end{array}$	$\begin{array}{r} 7 \\ -4 \\ \hline 2 \end{array}$
$\begin{array}{r} 9 \\ -6 \\ \hline 4 \end{array}$	$\begin{array}{r} 8 \\ -0 \\ \hline 8 \end{array}$	$\begin{array}{r} 8 \\ -1 \\ \hline 6 \end{array}$
$\begin{array}{r} 2 \\ -2 \\ \hline 1 \end{array}$	$\begin{array}{r} 5 \\ -3 \\ \hline 3 \end{array}$	$\begin{array}{r} 6 \\ -5 \\ \hline 1 \end{array}$

$\begin{array}{r} 9 \\ -1 \\ \hline 9 \end{array}$	$\begin{array}{r} 8 \\ -4 \\ \hline 3 \end{array}$	$\begin{array}{r} 8 \\ -8 \\ \hline 0 \end{array}$
$\begin{array}{r} 6 \\ -0 \\ \hline 0 \end{array}$	$\begin{array}{r} 4 \\ -2 \\ \hline 2 \end{array}$	$\begin{array}{r} 4 \\ -3 \\ \hline 2 \end{array}$
$\begin{array}{r} 7 \\ -5 \\ \hline 2 \end{array}$	$\begin{array}{r} 6 \\ -3 \\ \hline 2 \end{array}$	$\begin{array}{r} 7 \\ -2 \\ \hline 4 \end{array}$

70. Happy Hippos

Solve the math problems. Then hunt for the **difference** hidden in the picture.

10	18	6	9	14	17	8	16
7	2	3	0	5	4	2	0
−1	−7	−3	−3	−2	−1	−3	−6

My First Grade Workbook

71. Math Buzz

Solve each math problem. Then connect the dots **counting backward** from **10** to **1**.

$$\begin{array}{r} 17 \\ 5 \\ -3 \\ \hline \end{array}$$

$$\begin{array}{r} 13 \\ 3 \\ -2 \\ \hline \end{array}$$

$$\begin{array}{r} 18 \\ 6 \\ -5 \\ \hline \end{array}$$

$$\begin{array}{r} 15 \\ 4 \\ -1 \\ \hline \end{array}$$

$$\begin{array}{r} 11 \\ 1 \\ -4 \\ \hline \end{array}$$

$$\begin{array}{r} 19 \\ 8 \\ -6 \\ \hline \end{array}$$

$$\begin{array}{r} 8 \\ 3 \\ -4 \\ \hline \end{array}$$

$$\begin{array}{r} 7 \\ 0 \\ -5 \\ \hline \end{array}$$

$$\begin{array}{r} 19 \\ 14 \\ -2 \\ \hline \end{array}$$

$$\begin{array}{r} 12 \\ 7 \\ -1 \\ \hline \end{array}$$

72. Seashell Subtraction

Solve the math facts. Then use the color key to color the shells.

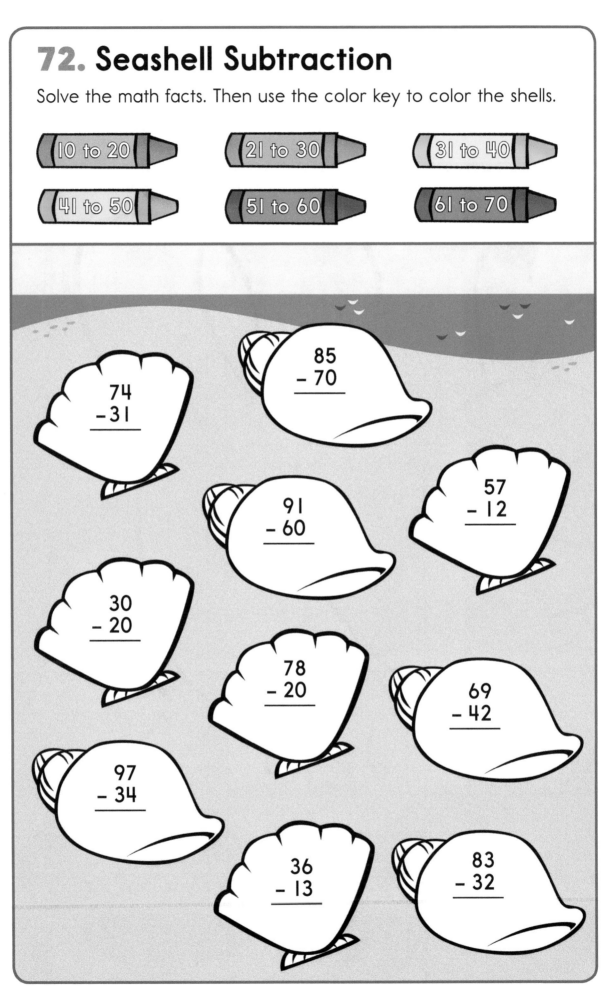

10 to 20

21 to 30

31 to 40

41 to 50

51 to 60

61 to 70

$$\begin{array}{r} 74 \\ -31 \\ \hline \end{array}$$

$$\begin{array}{r} 85 \\ -70 \\ \hline \end{array}$$

$$\begin{array}{r} 91 \\ -60 \\ \hline \end{array}$$

$$\begin{array}{r} 57 \\ -12 \\ \hline \end{array}$$

$$\begin{array}{r} 30 \\ -20 \\ \hline \end{array}$$

$$\begin{array}{r} 78 \\ -20 \\ \hline \end{array}$$

$$\begin{array}{r} 69 \\ -42 \\ \hline \end{array}$$

$$\begin{array}{r} 97 \\ -34 \\ \hline \end{array}$$

$$\begin{array}{r} 36 \\ -13 \\ \hline \end{array}$$

$$\begin{array}{r} 83 \\ -32 \\ \hline \end{array}$$

73. Crack the Cactus Code

Solve each subtraction problem. Then use the code to answer the riddle.

L
60
- 10

S
56
- 26

P
65
- 24

Y
35
- 21

A
97
- 32

R
84
- 11

U
78
- 15

T
96
- 73

O
93
- 72

K
87
- 35

M
28
- 13

H
48
- 22

What do you say to a fancy cactus?

Y __ __   __ __ __ __
14 21 63   50 21 21 52

__ __ __ __ __ .
30 26 65 73 41

74. Picnic at the Park

Solve the subtraction problems. Then trace a line through the correct path to the park.

$$\begin{array}{r} 20 \\ -\ 0 \\ \hline \end{array}$$

$$\begin{array}{r} 9 \\ -\ 8 \\ \hline \end{array}$$

$$\begin{array}{r} 12 \\ -\ 5 \\ \hline \end{array}$$

$$\begin{array}{r} 19 \\ -\ 2 \\ \hline \end{array}$$

$$\begin{array}{r} 15 \\ -\ 9 \\ \hline \end{array}$$

$$\begin{array}{r} 19 \\ -\ 1 \\ \hline \end{array}$$

$$\begin{array}{r} 11 \\ -\ 6 \\ \hline \end{array}$$

$$\begin{array}{r} 20 \\ -\ 1 \\ \hline \end{array}$$

$$\begin{array}{r} 17 \\ -\ 1 \\ \hline \end{array}$$

$$\begin{array}{r} 16 \\ -\ 3 \\ \hline \end{array}$$

$$\begin{array}{r} 19 \\ -\ 5 \\ \hline \end{array}$$

$$\begin{array}{r} 18 \\ -\ 3 \\ \hline \end{array}$$

$$\begin{array}{r} 5 \\ -\ 3 \\ \hline \end{array}$$

$$\begin{array}{r} 16 \\ -\ 7 \\ \hline \end{array}$$

$$\begin{array}{r} 17 \\ -\ 5 \\ \hline \end{array}$$

$$\begin{array}{r} 10 \\ -\ 7 \\ \hline \end{array}$$

$$\begin{array}{r} 15 \\ -\ 5 \\ \hline \end{array}$$

$$\begin{array}{r} 13 \\ -\ 3 \\ \hline \end{array}$$

$$\begin{array}{r} 19 \\ -\ 8 \\ \hline \end{array}$$

$$\begin{array}{r} 14 \\ -\ 6 \\ \hline \end{array}$$

75. Dinosaur Differences

Solve the math problems. Then use the color key to color the picture.

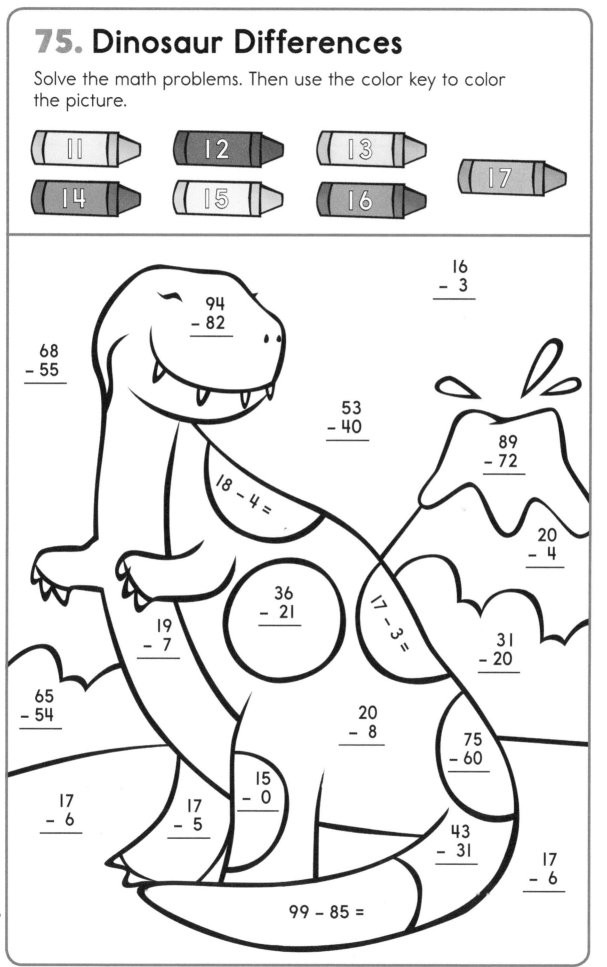

$$\begin{array}{r} 16 \\ -\ 3 \\ \hline \end{array}$$

$$\begin{array}{r} 94 \\ -\ 82 \\ \hline \end{array}$$

$$\begin{array}{r} 68 \\ -\ 55 \\ \hline \end{array}$$

$$\begin{array}{r} 53 \\ -\ 40 \\ \hline \end{array}$$

$$\begin{array}{r} 89 \\ -\ 72 \\ \hline \end{array}$$

$$18 - 4 =$$

$$\begin{array}{r} 20 \\ -\ 4 \\ \hline \end{array}$$

$$\begin{array}{r} 36 \\ -\ 21 \\ \hline \end{array}$$

$$17 - 3 =$$

$$\begin{array}{r} 19 \\ -\ 7 \\ \hline \end{array}$$

$$\begin{array}{r} 31 \\ -\ 20 \\ \hline \end{array}$$

$$\begin{array}{r} 65 \\ -\ 54 \\ \hline \end{array}$$

$$\begin{array}{r} 20 \\ -\ 8 \\ \hline \end{array}$$

$$\begin{array}{r} 75 \\ -\ 60 \\ \hline \end{array}$$

$$\begin{array}{r} 15 \\ -\ 0 \\ \hline \end{array}$$

$$\begin{array}{r} 17 \\ -\ 6 \\ \hline \end{array}$$

$$\begin{array}{r} 17 \\ -\ 5 \\ \hline \end{array}$$

$$\begin{array}{r} 43 \\ -\ 31 \\ \hline \end{array}$$

$$\begin{array}{r} 17 \\ -\ 6 \\ \hline \end{array}$$

$$99 - 85 =$$

76. Leafy Logic

Use the clues to help you color the leaves in the right order.

There is 1 green leaf, 1 brown leaf, 1 orange leaf, and 2 yellow leaves hanging on the branch.

The brown leaf is between 2 yellow leaves.

There is a green leaf on the end of the branch.

An orange leaf is to the left of the green leaf.

77. Fruity Facts

Look at the math problems. Can you figure out the value of each fruit?

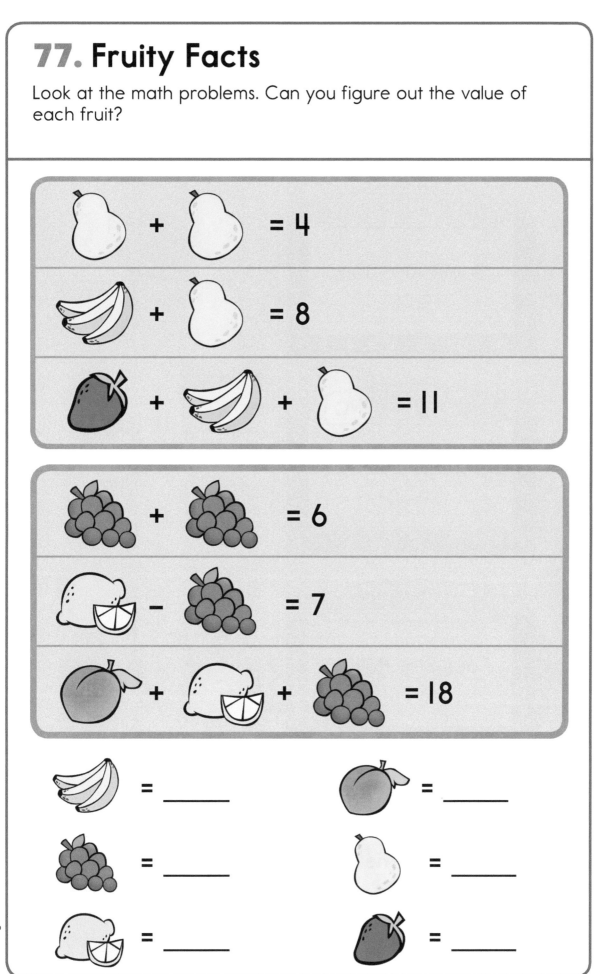

78. Showtime!

Draw a line to match the movie to its time. Then circle the movie you'd most like to see.

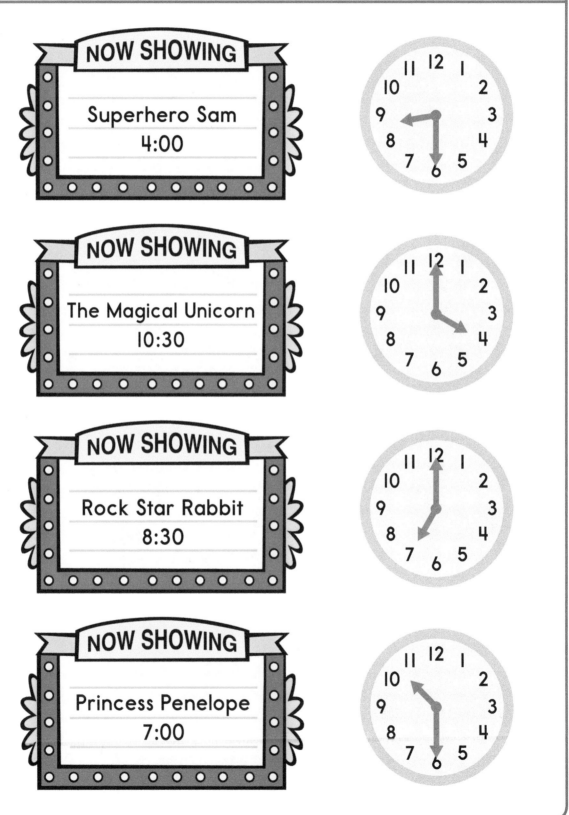

NOW SHOWING

Superhero Sam
4:00

NOW SHOWING

The Magical Unicorn
10:30

NOW SHOWING

Rock Star Rabbit
8:30

NOW SHOWING

Princess Penelope
7:00

79. Time to Match

Circle the analog clock in each row that matches the digital clock.

80. Let's Go Shopping!

Color the coins needed to buy each item.

My First Grade Workbook

81. How Much?

Count the money in each piggy bank. Draw a line to match each bank to the toy with that price.

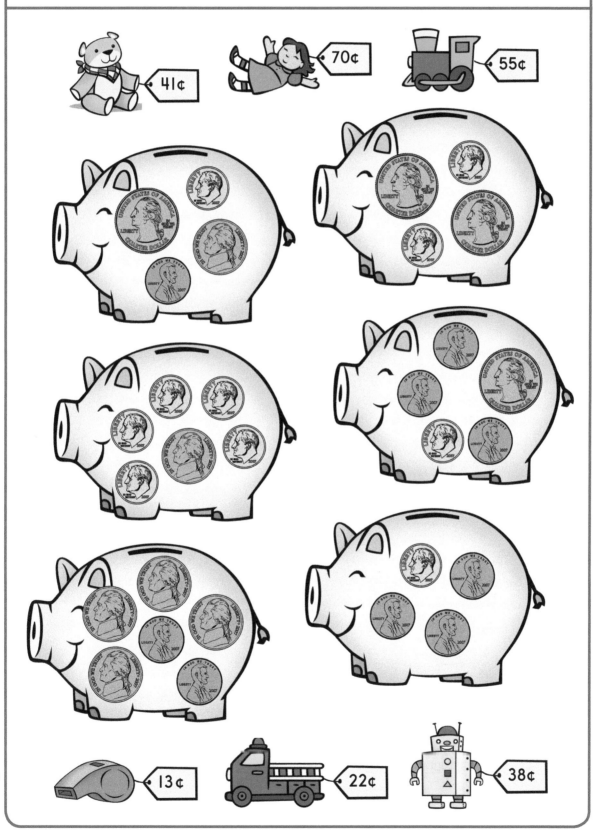

82. What's the Weather?

Solve the clues and complete the crossword puzzle. Use the word bank to help you.

Word Bank

windy   snowy   cloudy
foggy   sunny   rainy

Across →

4. During _____ weather, leaves blow around.

5. You cannot see the sun on a _____ day.

6. In _____ weather, it is hard to see far.

Down ↓

1. She likes to go to the beach when it is _____.

2. I need an umbrella when it is _____.

3. We need a coat, hat, and gloves when it is _____.

83. Scrambled Seasons

Unscramble the words. Then find them in the puzzle. Be sure to look across, down, and diagonally.

Word Bank
spring   summer   fall   winter   rain   leaves   sun   snow

tirnew _____   evlase _____

msurme _____   nus _____

lafl _____   irna _____

rpgins _____   wson _____

q	o	v	c	j	n	v	r	a	i	n	g
w	b	m	i	s	u	n	m	s	n	o	w
j	g	l	u	t	p	m	s	a	j	s	m
i	t	g	e	s	u	m	m	e	r	p	p
e	n	w	n	a	o	c	t	s	s	r	n
x	r	i	b	t	v	i	b	x	o	i	b
h	l	n	l	a	t	e	k	c	m	n	x
w	j	t	o	p	d	o	s	t	i	g	u
m	k	e	q	u	f	a	l	l	k	j	t
m	m	r	b	f	l	c	q	w	u	h	k
y	v	c	d	n	u	g	t	c	k	j	r
d	x	k	f	x	r	y	u	s	i	d	q

84. On the Farm

Circle **5** objects in the picture that are **non-living**.

My First Grade Workbook

85. Living Things in the Woods

Help Jack through the woods. Follow the path that has only **living** things.

86. How a Flower Grows

Show the life cycle of a flower. Draw a line from each picture to the correct circle.

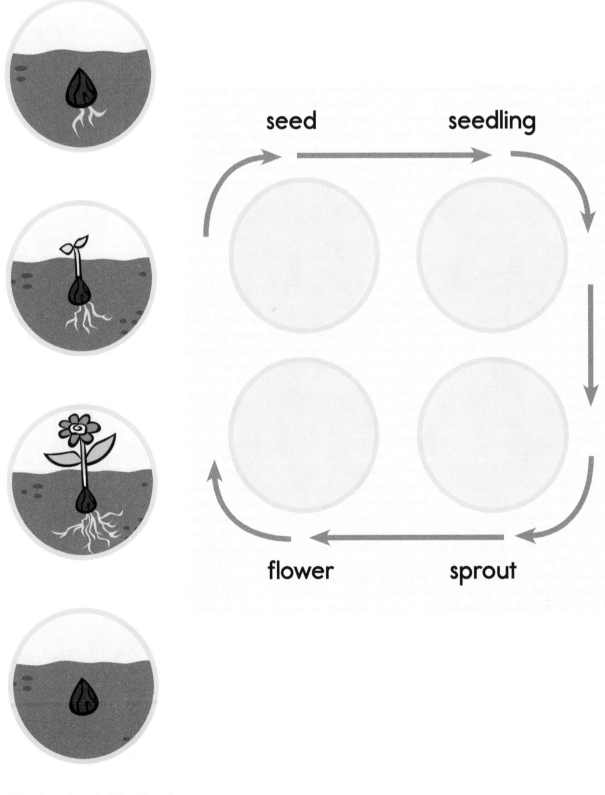

seed

seedling

flower

sprout

87. How a Frog Grows

Put these pictures in the right order. Write **1**, **2**, **3**, **4**, or **5** in the boxes to show the life cycle of a frog.

88. Solid or Liquid Lily Pads

Color the lily pads that have solid items on them **blue**. Color the lily pads that have liquid items on them **green**.

My First Grade Workbook

© Rockridge Press

89. Matter Match Up

Color each marble to match the jar it belongs in.

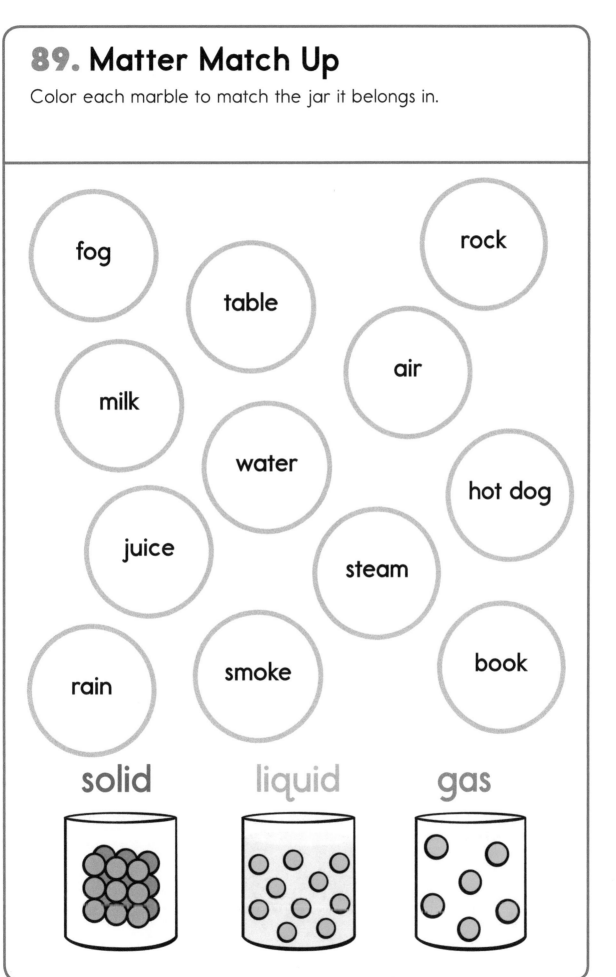

fog

rock

table

air

milk

water

hot dog

juice

steam

rain

smoke

book

solid   **liquid**   **gas**

90. When Does It Happen?

Look at each picture. Draw a line to show if it happens during the day or at night.

DAY

NIGHT

I go to sleep.

I go to school.

I eat dinner.

I get dressed.

I put on pajamas.

I eat breakfast.

My First Grade Workbook

© Rockridge Press

91. Day or Night?

Draw a 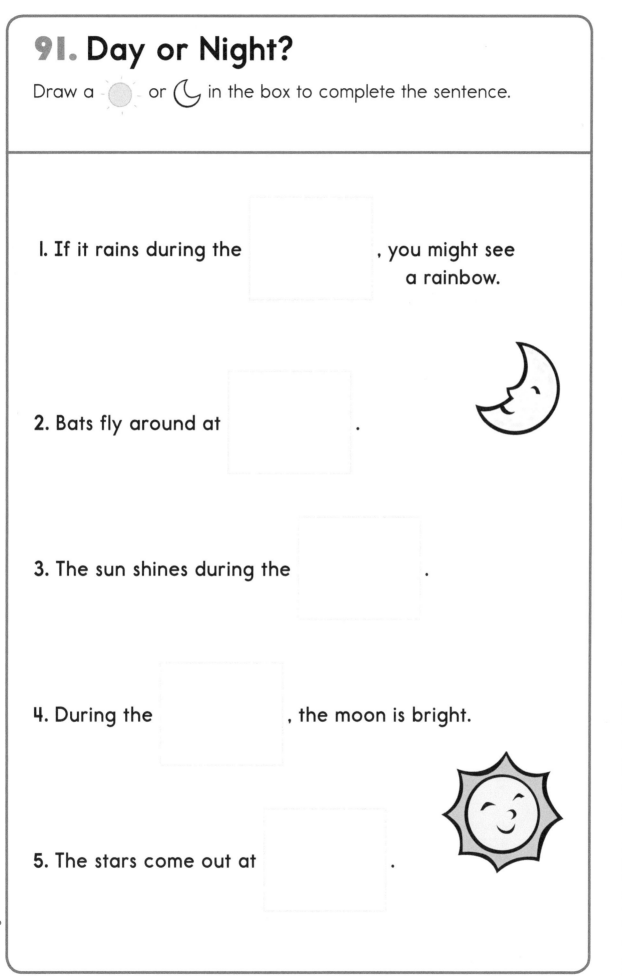 or ☾ in the box to complete the sentence.

1. If it rains during the ☐ , you might see a rainbow.

2. Bats fly around at ☐ .

3. The sun shines during the ☐ .

4. During the ☐ , the moon is bright.

5. The stars come out at ☐ .

92. Space Scramble

Unscramble the words. Then use the code to answer the riddle.

Word Bank

planet rocket comet galaxy
astronaut shuttle gravity

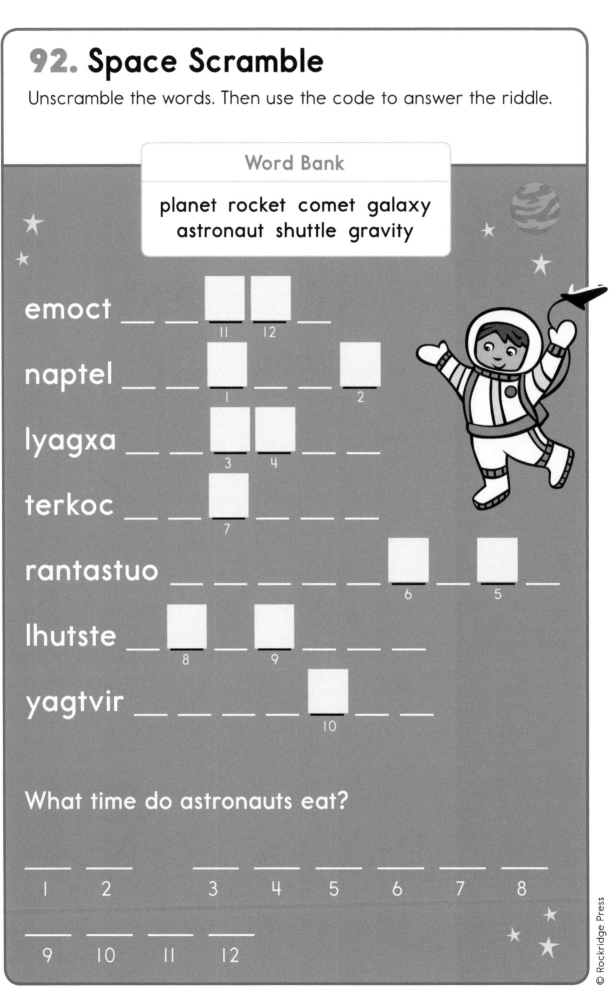

emoct __ __ __ __ __
　　　　　　11　12

naptel __ __ __ __ __ __
　　　　　　1　　　　　2

lyagxa __ __ __ __ __ __
　　　　　3　4

terkoc __ __ __ __ __ __
　　　　　　7

rantastuo __ __ __ __ __ __ __ __ __
　　　　　　　　　　　6　　　5

lhutste __ __ __ __ __ __ __
　　　　8　　9

yagtvir __ __ __ __ __ __ __
　　　　　　　　10

What time do astronauts eat?

__ __ __ __ __ __ __ __
1　2　　3　4　5　6　7　8

__ __ __ __
9　10　11　12

93. Searching the Solar System

Can you find all the planets? Look across, down, and diagonally to solve the puzzle.

Word Bank

Mercury Venus Earth Mars
Jupiter Saturn Uranus Neptune

o	u	o	c	q	i	r	o	d	s	k	k	s	e	c
s	r	t	b	q	x	g	o	u	m	h	o	s	k	e
r	a	o	s	p	c	a	n	i	i	g	x	u	e	m
a	n	z	a	q	a	e	k	e	c	s	n	n	s	h
e	u	j	t	u	v	m	i	l	p	s	m	p	j	g
o	s	y	u	k	q	c	o	d	z	t	h	k	a	g
g	z	a	r	p	o	k	u	q	d	t	u	h	m	v
s	v	j	n	p	i	a	f	y	r	f	o	n	x	y
o	x	b	f	x	y	t	q	a	k	l	g	g	e	j
p	j	x	l	y	x	w	e	p	b	u	s	z	x	a
m	a	h	r	y	v	z	s	r	s	z	d	y	u	c
a	v	u	d	s	b	r	a	i	x	h	t	a	d	w
i	c	x	r	p	f	v	m	e	r	c	u	r	y	j
v	a	a	a	a	c	u	m	t	j	u	m	f	v	o
e	m	f	b	k	s	r	s	n	y	e	x	g	m	c

94. In the Ocean

Circle the things you would find in the ocean. Put an X on the things that don't belong in the ocean. Three in a row makes tic-tac-toe!

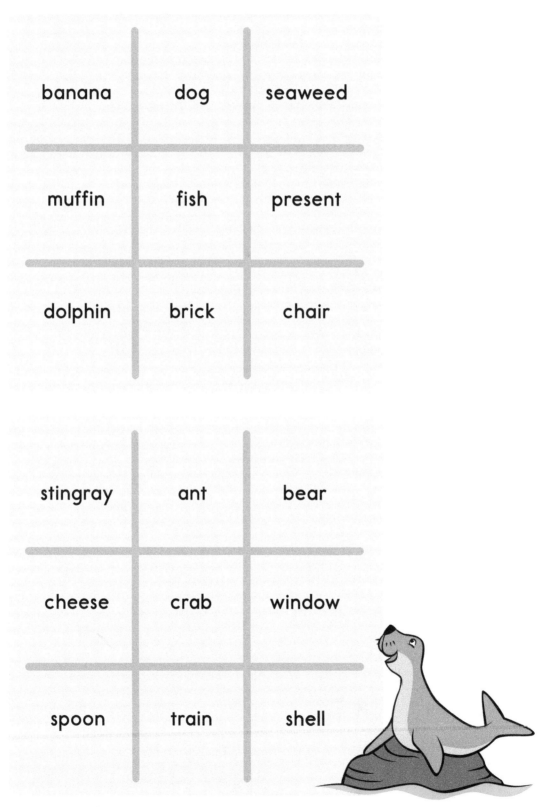

banana	dog	seaweed
muffin	fish	present
dolphin	brick	chair

stingray	ant	bear
cheese	crab	window
spoon	train	shell

My First Grade Workbook

95. Ocean Animals

Solve the clues and complete the crossword puzzle. Use the word bank to help you.

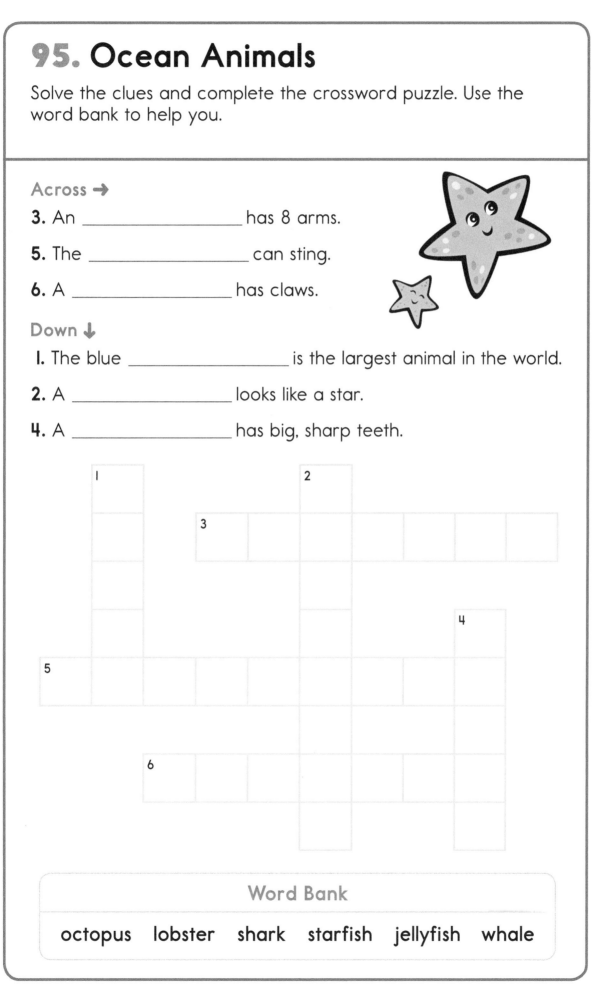

Across →

3. An _____ has 8 arms.

5. The _____ can sting.

6. A _____ has claws.

Down ↓

1. The blue _____ is the largest animal in the world.

2. A _____ looks like a star.

4. A _____ has big, sharp teeth.

Word Bank

octopus   lobster   shark   starfish   jellyfish   whale

96. All About Me

Answer the questions. Color the picture to look like you. Be sure to add the details!

What is your name?

_____

How old are you? _____

What grade are you in? _____

What is your favorite color?

_____

What is your favorite food?

_____

What is your favorite hobby or sport?

_____

What is your favorite book?

_____

What is your favorite movie?

_____

What do you want to be when you grow up?

_____

My First Grade Workbook

97. What Doesn't Belong?

Circle the tools each community helper needs to do their job. Put an ✗ on any objects the person does not need.

© Rockridge Press

98. Hunt for Community Helpers

Can you find all of the community helpers? Search across, down, and diagonally to solve the puzzle.

Word Bank

dentist librarian farmer veterinarian
judge banker mechanic pilot

w	e	f	m	n	z	t	x	y	z	w	y	p	t	c
r	i	t	v	n	o	l	z	w	a	q	e	f	i	b
r	q	r	v	l	k	c	x	r	i	g	c	n	b	u
m	m	g	i	d	v	y	t	v	d	o	a	h	m	m
x	l	p	s	e	e	j	e	u	o	h	p	s	p	y
u	i	u	b	n	t	a	j	i	c	q	k	f	v	t
z	b	p	e	t	e	y	i	e	w	z	l	b	r	o
k	r	x	i	i	r	y	m	x	n	t	a	e	c	q
f	a	p	j	s	i	n	v	q	v	a	k	f	d	d
u	r	u	y	t	n	z	k	f	d	n	p	m	u	s
n	i	m	o	j	a	z	e	t	a	z	m	w	s	y
j	a	o	d	z	r	m	d	b	y	r	c	f	o	c
k	n	g	p	g	i	f	a	r	m	e	r	t	w	t
r	i	q	c	c	a	r	p	u	g	w	o	e	v	e
n	c	p	i	a	n	i	z	e	p	e	w	f	r	l

My First Grade Workbook

99. Want or Need?

Decide if each word is a want or a need. Use the color key to color the picture.

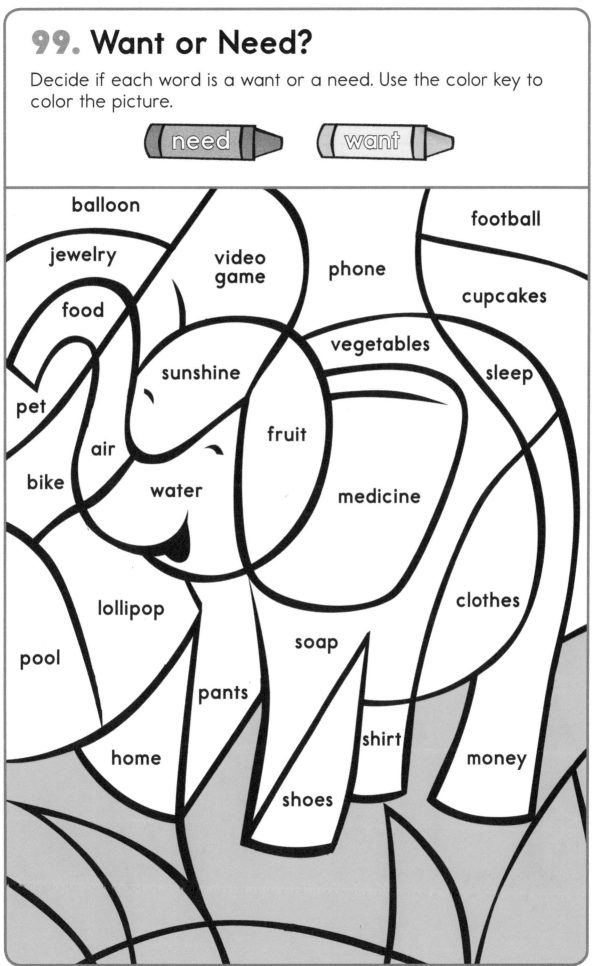

need   want

balloon

football

jewelry

video game

phone

food

cupcakes

vegetables

sunshine

sleep

pet

fruit

air

medicine

bike

water

clothes

lollipop

soap

pool

pants

shirt

home

money

shoes

100. Main Street Maze

Follow the directions to draw Olivia's path through town.
Then draw the details on the map.

Start

Main Street

SCHOOL

GAS STATION

Pine Avenue

1st Street

POST OFFICE

2nd Street

Maple Drive

Hill Drive

LIBRARY

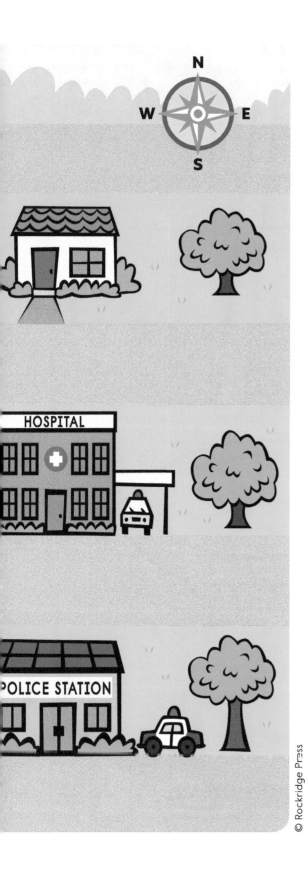

Directions

1. Olivia needs to go to the post office. To get there, she will walk **east** on Main Street and turn **south** onto 1st Street.

2. Now she wants to get a book. She will keep walking **south** on 1st Street and then turn **east** on Hill Drive to get to the library.

3. To go home, Olivia will go **north** on 2nd Street and then turn **east** onto Pine Avenue.

Details

1. Draw a car on the street that is on the **west** side of the gas station.

2. Circle the building that is to the **north** of the police station.

3. Draw 2 trees on the **east** side of the church.

4. Put an X on the building that is to the **south** of the school.

My First Grade Workbook

101. Pick Up on the Playground

Color the items that should be recycled **green**. Color the items that should go in the trash **red**.

Social Studies Skills **113**

Answer Key

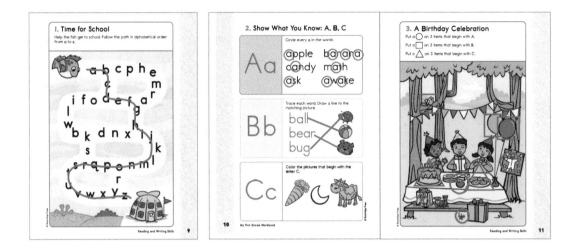

1. Time for School

Help the fish get to school. Follow the path in alphabetical order from a to z.

a b c p h e
c m
i f o d e f a r
g
w b k d n x j k
s h
s r q p o n m l
r
u v w x y z

2. Show What You Know: A, B, C

Circle every a in the words.

Aa

(a)pple ban(a)n(a)
c(a)ndy m(a)th
(a)sk (a)w(a)ke

Trace each word. Draw a line to the matching picture.

Bb

ball
bear
bug

Color the pictures that begin with the letter C.

Cc

3. A Birthday Celebration

Put a ○ on 3 items that begin with A.
Put a □ on 3 items that begin with B.
Put a △ on 3 items that begin with C.

4. Show What You Know: D, E, F

Circle every D or d.

Dd

(J) d z (D) (d)
(D) (d) r l (D)

Write the missing letter in each word.

Ee

__e__nvelope
__e__lephant
__e__gg

Unscramble the words. Each one begins with the letter F.

Ff

rfma __farm__
ofto __foot__
frei __fire__
afn __fan__

5. Be the Artist

Draw a picture on the easel that begins with the sound on the paint can.

Pictures will vary

6. Show What You Know: G, H, I

Circle every g in the words.

Gg

(g)oat (g)ame
le(g) wi(gg)le
(g)orilla pi(g)

Trace each word. Draw a line to the matching picture.

Hh

hat
house
heart

Color the pictures that begin with the letter I.

Ii

7. Let's Go Fishing!

Color the fish with uppercase letters purple. Color the fish with lowercase letters yellow.

a o W
h F J
B S t
X u Q
i m L

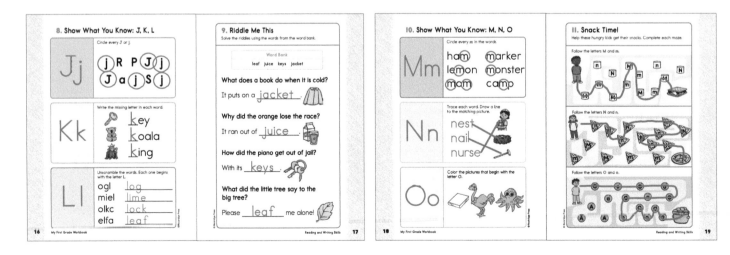

8. Show What You Know: J, K, L

Circle every J or j.

Jj

(j) R P (J) (j)
(J) a (j) S (j)

Write the missing letter in each word.

Kk

__k__ey
__k__oala
__k__ing

Unscramble the words. Each one begins with the letter L.

Ll

ogl __log__
miel __lime__
olkc __lock__
elfa __leaf__

9. Riddle Me This

Solve the riddles using the words from the word bank.

Word Bank
leaf juice keys jacket

What does a book do when it is cold?

It puts on a __jacket__ .

Why did the orange lose the race?

It ran out of __juice__ .

How did the piano get out of jail?

With its __keys__ .

What did the little tree say to the big tree?

Please __leaf__ me alone!

10. Show What You Know: M, N, O

Circle every m in the words.

Mm

ha(m) (m)arker
le(m)on (m)onster
(m)o(m) ca(m)p

Trace each word. Draw a line to the matching picture.

Nn

nest
nail
nurse

Color the pictures that begin with the letter O.

Oo

11. Snack Time!

Help these hungry kids get their snacks. Complete each maze.

Follow the letters M and m.

Follow the letters N and n.

Follow the letters O and o.

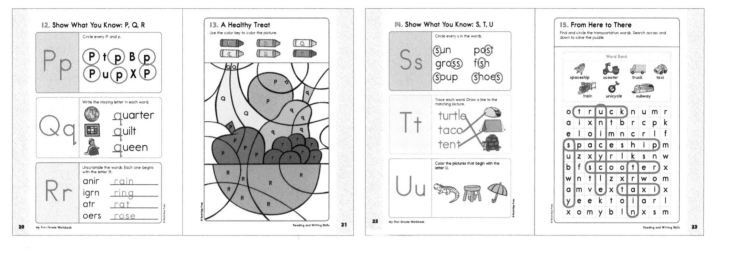

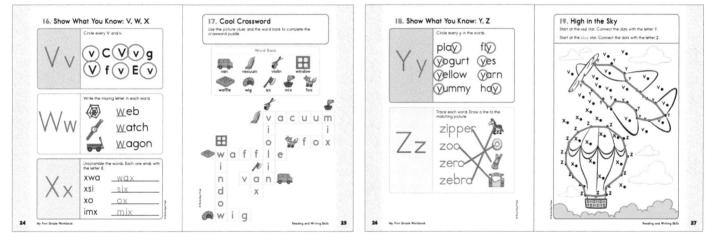

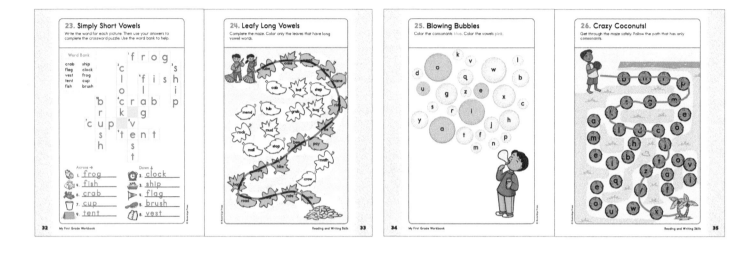

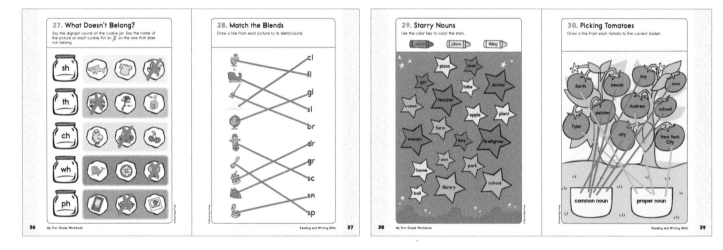

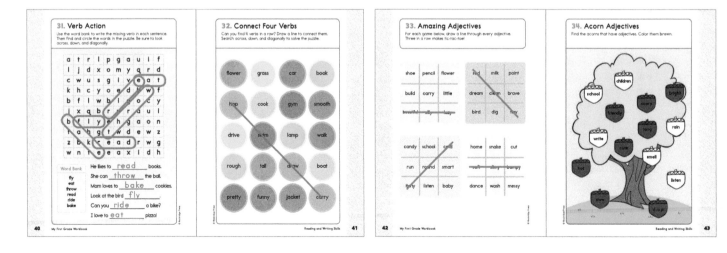

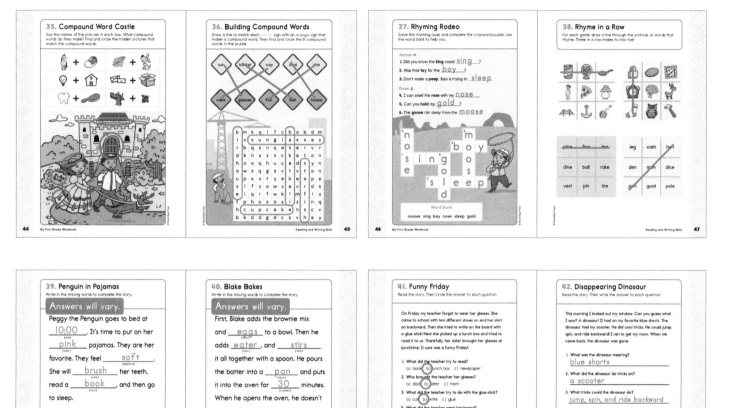

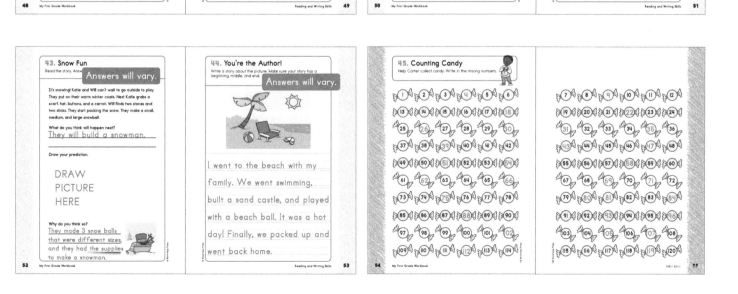

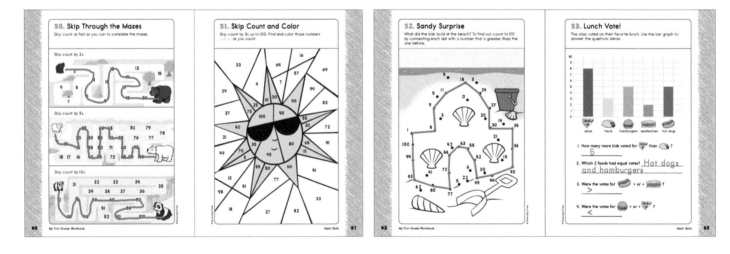

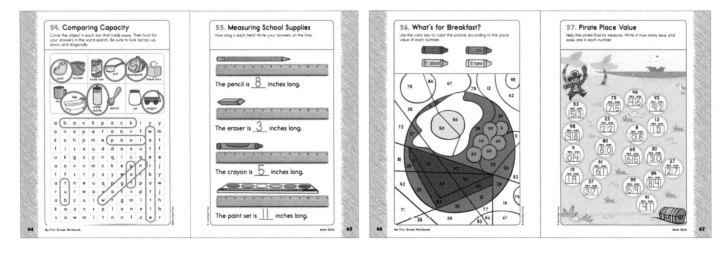

118 Answer Key

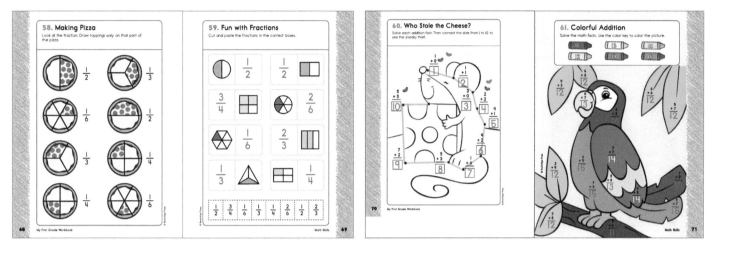

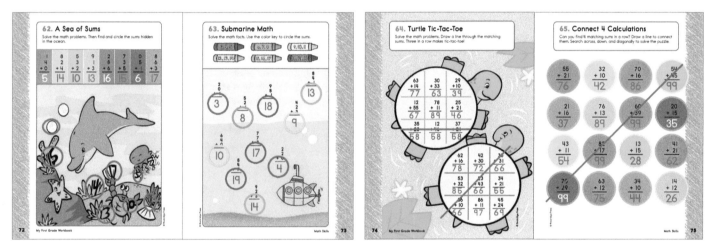

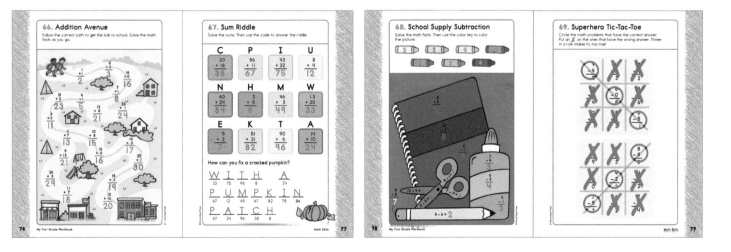

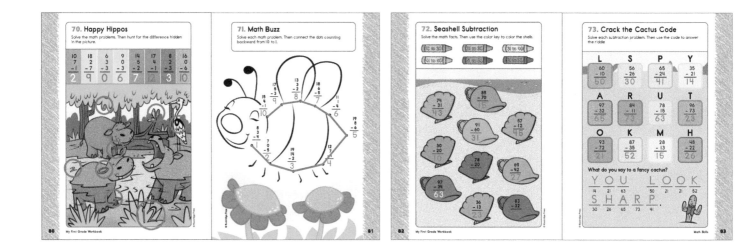

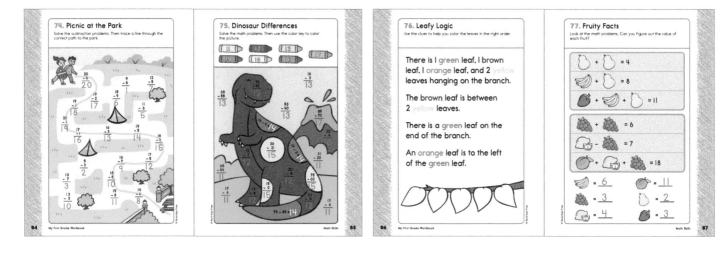

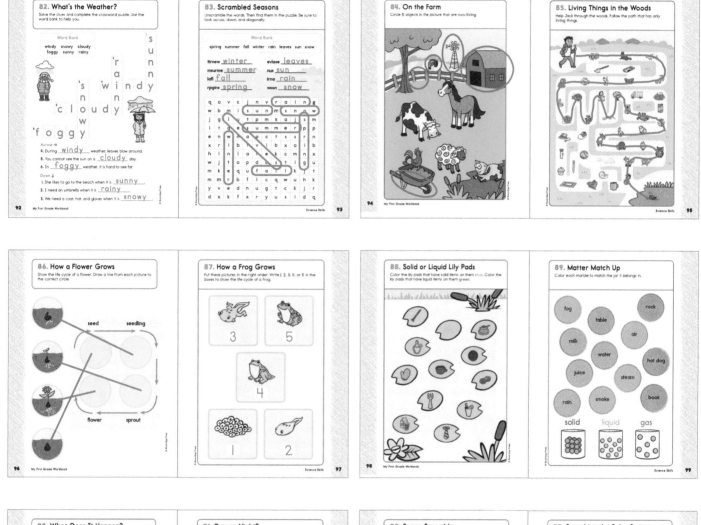

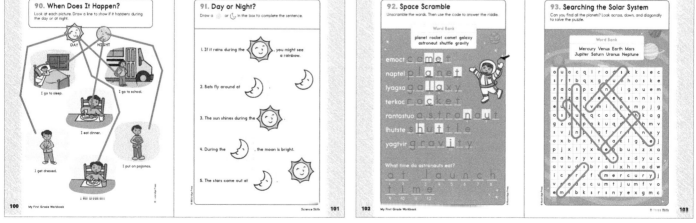

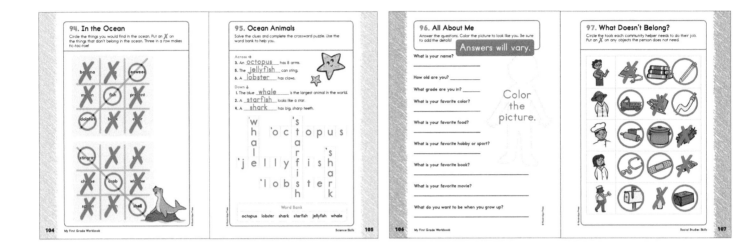

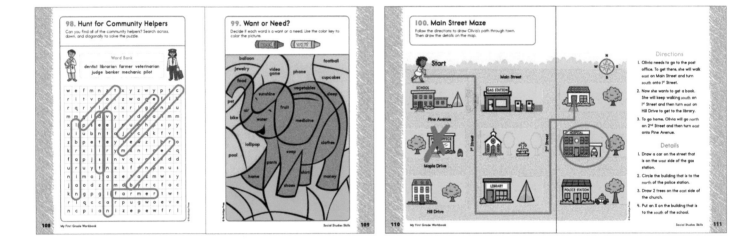

About the Author

Brittany Lynch holds a bachelor's degree in elementary education and a master's degree in early childhood education. After teaching in the primary grades for eight years, she now works as a curriculum author, providing resources for elementary teachers around the world. Brittany loves to incorporate technology into learning and create hands-on, engaging resources that make learning fun. She is also the author of *My Kindergarten Workbook*.

Brittany lives in Florida with her husband and dog. In her free time, she enjoys reading, traveling, shopping, and going to the beach.

Visit www.tickledpinkinprimary.com to find out more about her work.

CONGRATULATIONS!

_____

(your name)

has completed all the activities in

My First Grade Workbook.

YOU'RE A FANTASTIC FIRST GRADER!

Continue the Learning Fun!

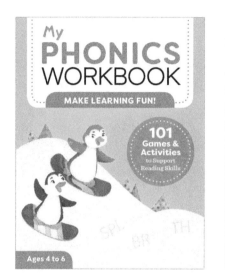

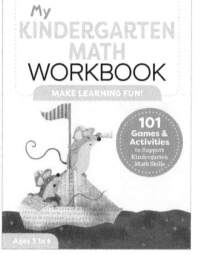

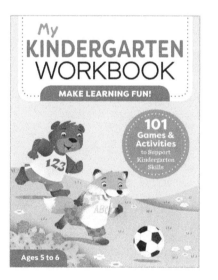

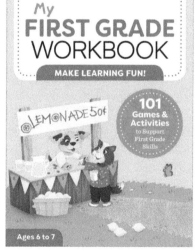